The Naked Australian

Australia, Her People, and the Way They Live

by

Brian Lewis

A/A Publishing, Carmichael, California

THE NAKED AUSTRALIAN
Australia, Her People, And The Way They Live

By Brian Lewis

A/A Publishing
Post Office Box 1772
Carmichael, Ca. 95609

Copyright 1987 by Brian Lewis
Printed in The United States of America

10 9 8 7 6 5 4 3 2 1

Library of Congress Catalog Card Number
86–072287

ISBN 0–940749–00–9 Paperback
ISBN 0–940749–02–5 Hardcover

ACKNOWLEDGMENTS

First and foremost I would like to thank my wife, Bonnie Redgrave–Lewis, who was a widow to my manuscript and computer for much of the two years it took to prepare this book. Without her support and encouragement this book project would not have been possible.

I am deeply indebted to Mr. Alonzo E. Meyer, without whose fine editing this work would not be of such a high standard.

Thanks to Mr. Peter McLaughlin, Editorial Manager of The Melbourne Age, who gave permission for the reproduction of many articles that appear throughout this work.

Thanks to Mr. Ron Tandberg, Cartoonist, whose work appears throughout this book, in helping me express ideas in other than words.

Thanks to Mr. Roger Johnstone, Editor of Australian Business Magazine, for permission to reproduce material.

Thanks to Mr. Tom Durbrow, Consulting Engineer, for his instruction and guidance on computer equipment during the preparation of this work.

Thanks to Susan Curry of The Australian Book Source, Davis, California.

Finally I would like to thank the people of Australia, past and present. They are responsible for providing the subject matter that made this project so worthwhile.

TABLE OF CONTENTS

3

Chapter Four continued

Chapter Five
BUSINESS IN AUSTRALIA

Chapter Six
CONSUMERISM

Chapter Seven
THE AUSTRALIAN GOVERNMENT

Chapter Eight
SOCIAL SECURITY & THE SAFETY NET

Chapter Nine
TAXES

Chapter Nine continued...

Chapter Ten
SCHOOLS IN AUSTRALIA

Chapter Eleven
HOUSING

Chapter Twelve
CRIME & PUNISHMENT IN AUSTRALIA

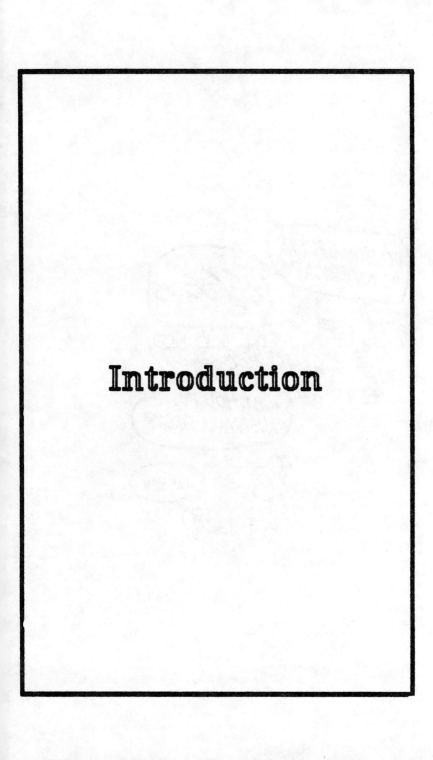

Introduction

What do rock groups: Men At Work and Little River Band; solo artists: Olivia Newton–John and Rick Springfield; movies: Crocodile Dundee and The Man from Snowy River; the books made into T.V. movies: The Thorn Birds and A Town Like Alice; actors Paul Hogan and Brian Brown; the sport of Australian Rules Football and Aussie Bear and Cherry Ripe candy bars all have in common? Jointly they are responsible for the current rage in interest about all things Australian, and for causing more Americans than ever to visit Australia in recent years.

In the past few years, America has developed an insatiable appetite for contemporary Australian culture. As an expatriate Australian living in Northern California with my American born wife since 1981, it has never ceased to amaze me how sincerely interested Americans are in Australia. It is as though there is no end to their interest in that land of wonder, Down Under.

The most likely reason that you would read this book is that you too are caught up in the 'mystery' of Australia. The desire to know more about Australia is based largely on innocent ignorance and popular misconceptions about life in Australia. Millions of Americans have been subjected to decades of glimpses, insights and stories about Australia. You may have been lucky enough to visit Australia at some time or doubtless you know someone who has. One thing is more than certain, that is, before this book, everything Americans have heard, seen and read about Australia has been very carefully calculated, leaving one with an impression that Australia must be some kind of 'paradise on earth'. While every country is guilty to some extent of presenting a somewhat less than truthful image to the rest of the world, Australia's efforts in this regard I believe border on the fantastic.

9

You may have seen a National Geographic T.V. show that investigates Australia's unique flora and fauna. You may know someone who has been to Australia for a vacation or spent some time there during World War II, the Korean or Vietnam wars, on R&R in the service, and heard the glowing reports these transient visitors give about the people and lifestyle in Australia. This type of input over the last forty years has generated a very sincere desire by many Americans to visit Australia. Since 1981 I have yet to meet any American who did not express a sincere interest in Australia; the land, the people or its current flood of entertainment offerings.

In contrast to what Americans have been indoctrinated with concerning Australia, in fact it is a place of strange social contrasts, especially as it looks and feels at first to the American visitor like a different, less populated and dated America. A better place? A new frontier? A dream never realized?

It is precisely because of the overwhelming amount of misinformation about Australia that I decided to write this book. For far too long the Australian Government, through its embassies and the Australian Tourist Commission, has been responsible for perpetuating an international image of Australia of years gone by.

It is time to set the record straight! Throughout this easily read and understood book you will be exposed to the real Australia. You will be able to make comparisons between your own life in America and the way it really is in the Land of Aus (pronounced OZ).

Chapter One

Australia: The Land

AUSTRALIA

* is physically almost the same size as the continental United States (2,966,200 sq. ml. Aus., 3,623,420 sq. ml. U.S.)
* is the sixth largest country after the Soviet Union, Canada, China, The U.S. and Brazil.
* has 22,959 miles of coast line.
* is one of the earth's oldest land masses.
* is the flattest of all continents.
* has an average height above sea level of approximately 950 feet compared to the rest of the world's average 2200 feet above sea level.
* is approximately 7,000 feet above sea level at its highest point.
* is the driest continent after Antarctica.
* has 230 species of native mammals, 300 of lizard, 140 of snake, two of crocodile and about 800 bird species.
* is the only nation to occupy an entire continent.
* has six states and two territories.
* has approximately 16 million people.

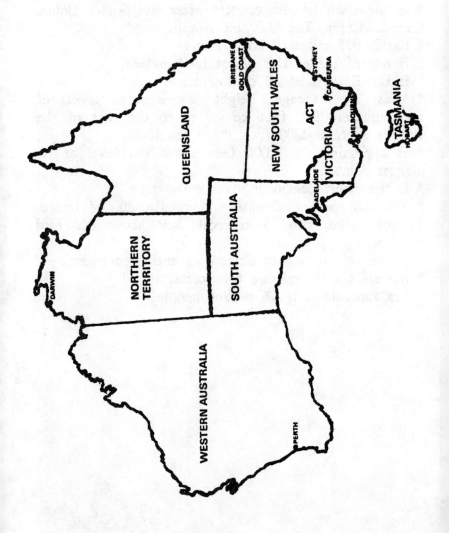

Fig 1. Australia - The Land.

How Victorians compare with their cousins in the other States

Western Australia:
Least rates paid per head of population ($73).
Highest proportion of motor vehicles (563 per 1000 people).
Greatest number of immigrants (in Perth).
Highest proportion of population in prison (1 per 1000 people).

Northern Territory:
Lowest proportion of childless families.
Least populated place in Australia.
Most beer drunk per head of population (23.6 litres for each person a year).
Greatest annual increase in population over past 50 years (more than 7 per cent a year on average).
Highest proportion of single-parent families (more than 11 per cent).
Highest birthrate in Australia: 50 per cent higher than in Victoria.

Queensland:
Highest population of Aborigines and Torres Strait Islanders.
Highest incidence of road fatalities: 2.4 deaths per 10,000 people.
Fewest telephones per head of population: 44.5 per 100.
Highest proportion of hospital beds: 6.8 per 1000 people.
More spent per head of population on Parliament ($10 for each Queenslander).

Australian Capital Territory:
Greatest population density: 97 persons per square kilometre (compared with 1 person per 10 square kilometres in NT).
Most divorces per head of population: more than twice the national average.
Most highly educated populace: more university graduates and people with doctorates, proportionately, than anywhere else in Australia.

South Australia:
Highest proportion of childless families.
Highest proportion of people with no post-school qualifications.

New South Wales:
Most populous State: more than one in three Australians, or almost 5.5 million people live in NSW. (A little over a quarter live in Victoria.)
Fewest public servants per head of population (90 per 1000 citizens).
Largest number of New Zealanders — Sydney has the fifth biggest population of Kiwis in the world.

Victoria:
Smallest proportion of single-parent families (6 per cent of all families).
Greatest proportion of non-English speaking immigrants (in Melbourne).
Most educated populace (apart from those in the ACT): nearly one in four Victorians older than 20 have had 10 or more years of schooling.
Most daily newspapers sold in Australia (more than 1 million) and Victorians, proportionately, read more newspapers than anyone else in the country.
Most telephones: 59 telephones per 100 people.

Tasmania:
Smallest proportion of population (40 per cent) live in capital city or in towns of less than 100,000 people.
Lowest incidence of syphilis (0.2 cases per 100,000 people).
Lowest proportion of swimming pools (50 per 1000 households).

Fig 2
(Courtesy of The Melbourne Age)

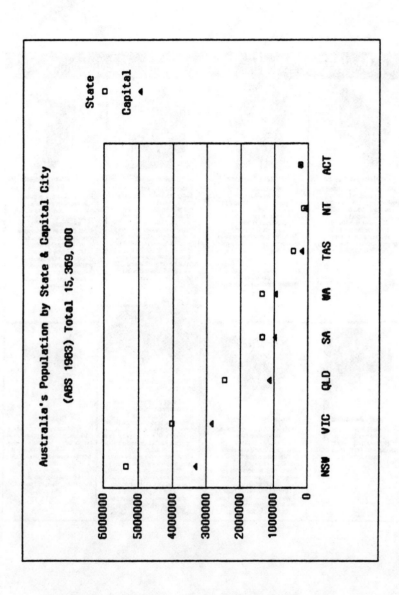

Fig 3.   Australia's Population

Chapter Two

A
Brief
History

This book will not bore you with a long and drawn out account of Australia's history. It is appropriate, however, to relate certain facts of Australian history, particularly those that are relevant to current conditions inside Australia. The following is therefore only a very cursory view of Australia's past.

DISCOVERY AND SETTLEMENT

European explorers came in contact with the Australian continent in the 1600's. Most were not interested in this strange land mass so far from their home port. Dutch sailor Dirk Hartog sailed up the west coast and found little more than 2,000 miles of desert. Hartog turned for home and reported very little of interest to the Dutch authorities.

In the late 1700's however, Captain James Cook of The Royal Navy and of Hawaiian history fame, laid claim to Australia for Britain. The British had the good fortune to begin their exploration of Australia from the east coast, finding a large expanse of habitable land near what is present day Sydney. The British government thought that Australia would provide a good site for a convict colony, situated 12,000 miles from Britain, and requiring six months travel time, there would be little likelyhood of escapees returning to the British Isles. In 1788 the occupation of Australia began in earnest with the arrival of The First Fleet. Unlike the American pilgrims, this band of settlers consisted of convicts, sailors and the military personnel. For all intents and purposes there was little difference between each group of these 'New Australians'. As they were all 12,000 miles from home, every man had to suffer the difficulties of a new uncivilized land. Australian history books are full of accounts that graphically depict the death and disease that commonly haunted these early voyages to Australia. It wasn't long before the potential of Australia was realized, and as

13

favorable reports flowed back to Britain a steady flow of free settlers made the long voyage to the new colony. If these daring free settlers made it to the shores of Australia, many of them shared quite handsomely in the abundance of this new land. As convicts were released after serving their time and soldiers chose civilian life rather than re-enlistment, the civilian population grew rapidly. By the mid 1800's Australia had begun to take on a character all its own: a nation unified by the challenge of carving out a new and great land, and hoping to be free from many of the injustices and inequalities of their British homeland.

THE ABORIGINES

When the early navigators arrived in Australia they encountered very dark skinned natives most of whom were quite passive. For want of a more exact description these natives were dubbed 'Aborigines', probably history's first real use of a generic term. Compared to other South Pacific natives encountered by Captain Cook and other explorers, the Aborigines seemed to be much more primitive, living in a stone age culture. Anthropologists believe that the Aborigines migrated from Asia when the Australian and Asian land masses were connected, about 40,000 years ago.

It is not hard to imagine the impact of the white man on these primitive people. Disaster was written on every tree. The Aborigines were a nomadic tribal people with no crop growing or animal herding to fall back on if their food gathering life style was interfered with to any significant degree. As the small extended family tribe was their mainstay, they did not have the ability to join forces and battle the encroachment of the whiteman. Aborigines were both incapable, and relatively uninterested in adjusting to this new lifestyle being established about them.

As their hunting grounds and waterholes were taken over for use by cattle and sheep and their sacred environment cleared to grow the white man's crops, they began to suffer a rapid decline. The settlers even went to the extreme of exterminating the Tasmanian Aborigines, a separate and distinct race from the mainland natives. This sad event is often conveniently forgotten when Australians talk about how badly other ex-colonies treat their natives and how America had treated its black population for years.

Today the Australian Aboriginie is fighting a battle similar to that of the American Indian, making a desperate attempt to save his unique culture and identity.

Will the tourist see Aborigines when he visits Australia? If he goes to the 'Outback', to Alice Springs or to Ayer's Rock he will see Aborigines. He will also most likely see them living in very sub-standard conditions in 'humpies' or in tin shacks in the desert or in abandoned cars. When Australians proudly say they do not have slums or ghettos like the United States, they conveniently forget about the way many Aborigines live in Australia. For what ever reasons, after 200 years the white Australian majority still has difficulty in dealing with the Aboriginal population in realistic terms. It is as though the caucasians really do not want to solve the problems facing the Aborigines' cultural, spiritual and economic needs.

COLONIAL GROWTH

As the colony of Australia grew rapidly in the 1800's, it soon became socially and economically quite different from its parent Britain. Ex-convicts and discharged military personnel, as well as free settlers of previously very little means, were able to become quite wealthy and hold high social and government positions, unheard of in mainstream British society. The Australian people did consider themselves different from their British counterparts as Australians shared a great vision of a country with a rich future for coming generations. Hand in hand with this great vision came a desire to be rid of the oppressive British parent that still held a tight control over all activities of the colony. This, however, while true in some aspects, is undermined by the fact that even today the British influence in all aspects of life is quite overwhelming.

The agricultural bounty of Australia was well exploited by the mid 1800's when someone, an American I believe, discovered gold in Victoria. As with all gold rushes of that time, the cities soon lost a large part of their populations as people flooded the 'diggings' to make their fortune. Of course the businessmen and women were on the gold fields as well to share in the new found wealth. It didn't take long for the colonial government to formulate some way to tax these people "about to get rich". As all British colonies have experienced, the British Government has always been tax-happy, taking advantage of any situation to keep its subjects in line by economic oppression first and brute force second. The Victorian authorities decided to require a gold mining license for everyone who dug for gold. The fee had to be paid monthly regardless of whether or not any gold was extracted. The miners, or 'Diggers' as they became known, didn't take too kindly to this outrageous form of taxation. The license fee itself was set unrealistically high and was raised regularly. The license checking raids on the diggers by the local police and the military could be compared these days to Boarder Patrol/INS raids on farms in search of illegal aliens. The difference, however, is that the gold license inspection raids were so persistent and brutal that they caused one of the few open rebellions in Australia's history. The story of this rebellion, known as The Eureka Stockade, has been immortalized in book and film.

This event ended in the untimely death of some diggers and soldiers, and eventually changed the licensing procedures for gold miners. Born from this event was a flag, 'The Southern Cross', today a sign of contempt for British rule and influence in Australian life. This flag is actually flown over many city halls in Australia, in place of the Australian flag, to show outright defiance of the Australian monarchy. Yes, the reigning monarch of Great Britain is also the monarch of Australia. (See Figure 4)

CREATION OF THE AUSTRALIAN COMMONWEALTH

By the end of the 1800's, Australia's population and economy had grown enough to consider federation. Federation came in 1901. Although everything generally associated with federation was present – constitution, governments and courts – and Australia was gaining its nationhood, the future of Australia would change very little for those who expected to be free of British rule and influence. Britain always leaves its institutions and infrastructure with all ex-colonies if they don't make a clean break as a republic. What was delivered to the people of Australia seemed to be an independent and self-ruling nation. On the contrary, there was delivered a country that was still in the solid grip of all things British and it remains so until the present day.

Cleverly contrived, the executive power of government, both federal and state, was left in the hands of the Governor General and the State Governors. These individuals are not elected but appointed by the British sovereign upon the recommendations of the British and Australian governments. The power of the governor general was clearly displayed in 1975 when he conspired with the Chief Justice of the Australian High Court and Leader of the Federal Opposition, to dismiss all elected representatives in both federal houses of parliament. The equivalent American act would be if The President had the power to dismiss The United States Congress from office and call another election at any time! This clearly shows that the Australian citizen's vote really means nothing when it comes down to the bottom line.

AUSTRALIANS AT WAR

As a colony and a member of the British Commonwealth, Australia has been asked, or more accurately, obliged to enter numerous wars in support of British causes. The first war of note was The Boer War in South Africa (1899-1902). The British had a difficult time fighting the Boers, Dutch settlers turned separatists, who had taken up arms against British rule in their adopted land. The Boers employed guerrilla tactics to successfully resist the British troops in the environs of the 'bush'. British military leaders realized that the Australians and Boers were very similar in nature, rugged types, and that the terrain of South Africa was similar in many ways to Australia. As a result, Australian troops were sent to South Africa to do the Briton's work under British command, a situation that has never proved satisfactory. The Australians fought hard but the inevitable happened. The British command sent unofficial word that there were to be no military or civilian prisoners, all those captured must be shot, thus doing battle the same way as the Boers. The news of this situation reached the British and colonial press and there was a public outcry. The thought that civilized British and Australian troops were following a barbaric procedure of not taking prisoners was unacceptable. The British command responded by denying they ever suggested such a thing, and the

Fig 4
(Courtesy of The Melbourne Age)

THE AGE, Friday 6 February 1981

It began with an ad in 'The Age'.

The Norwegian couple asked for

information

about

Australia.

And ROBERT HAUPT

couldn't help but reply.

Fig 5a
(Courtesy of The Melbourne Age)

6 YES, Vivi, there is an Australia. Pour me a cup of tea and I'll tell you about it. Stop me if I go too fast.

First of all, look out the window at Norway. All snow and fir trees, right? Blizzards and reindeer. Well, Australia is nothing like that. If you hear us singing about dashing through the snow on a one-horse open sleigh, we are just pretending to be joyful, and you should pay no attention to it. Norway is steep and cold. Australia is hot and flat.

Much the same goes for the people. Please don't take this personally, but the Scandinavian temperament is, well, you know, a bit earnest, is it not, even perhaps a mite gloomy? Maybe it's the long winter, but your average Lapp or Lett takes a rather serious view of life. Let me tell you, Vivi, your average Australian doesn't.

By and large, your Australian does not take out newspaper advertisements seeking views on countries he proposes to shift to. It is not that he would think it a bad idea, but with all the other things he must attend to — has he packed the teapot? Will there be Vegemite? — he would just not get around to it.

If you put the human race in a line stretching from the Germans, who get everything done, to, say, the inhabitants of Belize, who get almost nothing done at all, the Australians would come in no better than half way.

We would not, for instance, sit in this industriousness index anywhere near the Norwegians, of whom the 'Encyclopaedia Britannica' says: "Men and women work hard in both town and country and recreation is often also strenuous".

This would be the last description you would use of the Australians.

The encyclopaedia goes on to note, of Norway, that mountain walking is a common pastime. Well, over the past few years it's really dropped right off in popularity in Australia, I'm afraid, along with mountain running, mountain strolling and every other division of mountain activity apart from paying a king's ransom to be towed up one side in order to slide down the other, which is probably something you are fairly bored with over there.

Australia is a cosmopolitan country: we have British trade unions, Italian planning, Russian bureaucracy and Irish politics. Even our railway lines . exhibit whimsical variety, each system incompatible with the others. In some parts of the country it's illegal to hold a meeting without permission. In others, to march. Everyone who comes to Australia has to be sprayed. I said sprayed, Vivi.

The difficulties all this causes us are without end. The cost in human misery, if you stop to think about it, is appalling. As I write this, I am wondering how my children are — I have two little daughters, too — because the schoolteachers are on strike.

We spend a fortune on gambling and alcohol, we have air

Fig 5b
(Courtesy of The Melbourne Age)

pollution, crime is getting worse and we have our own bitter little heroin scene. And for some reason, our telephone system doesn't work properly any more.

I'll get on to Australia's problem in a moment, but first let me try to explain to you why Australians are friendly, generous, shy and wonderful. How you can recognise them on a crowded street anywhere in the world by their open faces and slightly rolling walk. How it's a point of deep principle to help a friend. That it is a birthright to be given a "go".

This "go" of which I speak — how can I explain it to you? It is the chance to have a suck of the saveloy of life. You know, to get in for your chop, to put your snout into the trough and emerge with the froth of satisfaction on your lip. Got it?

Incidentally, if you come here, your children will be talking like this inside six months. They, too, will come to demand a fair go. If they don't get it — and, sadly, not all Australians get it — they will say it is a fair cow. But maybe I am confusing you.

And our problem? Isolation. You might not understand it, up there on the Arctic Circle, at the crossroads of culture, the hub of the world, but we are a very long way away. We are so far away, in fact, that no one has ever invaded our country, apart from us.

There is plenty of antagonism and disillusionment here, but there is no real fear. In the Great Australian Whinge — a cry of complaint as Australian as a yodel is Swiss — there is a note of self-satisfaction. Things are crook (bad), but every Australian knows they could be worse.

So if you don't mind your children speaking a language apparently devised for retarded cockatoos, and shrieking "Aw, gee, mum, give us a go" whenever you make a demand on them that would be the soul of reasonableness in Norway, you should come on down.

The water's fine.

Fig 5c
(Courtesy of The Melbourne Age)

military began to look for scapegoats on who to lay blame for some of these reported atrocities. The British court-marshalled and executed two Australian soldiers to put a close to this embarrassing situation. This particularly sad incident was recently portrayed in the widely acclaimed movie 'Breaker Morant".

The Australians also fought in the First World War under British command and were slaughtered along with other allied troops on the beaches of Galipoli. The Second World War produced a different approach to the situation. It was finally conceded that Australian troops would perform best under Australian command, so most theaters of war saw Australian commanders in charge of their own troops. The Australian soldier became known as a 'Digger', an obvious referral to the rugged gold mining days of Australia's past, and established a distinct identity among the allied troops. Australian soldiers gained a reputation for fighting hard and could be relied upon to act heroically in the toughest situations. There was some participation in the Korean War by Australian troops also.

The latest war involvement for Australian troops was of course Vietnam. There is an ironic twist to the current thinking about the U.S. involvement in the Vietnam war. It was reported in Australia in 1984 that it was Australia who asked the U.S. to become involved militarily in Vietnam. Apparently the Vietnam situation weighed heavily on the Australian Prime Minister at the time, and he called upon the U.S. as Australia's ally, to intercede on the regions behalf. After consultation with Vietnam the U.S. obliged. It would seem that Australia's hands are not as clean in regard to the Vietnam war as they would like the rest of the world to believe. While Australia's troop commitment to Vietnam was not as vast as the U.S., Australia lost 500 young men to that war.

It was also reported that Australia was poised to join Britain in its military action against Argentina over the Faulkland Islands. I had independent confirmation of an Australian soldier who claimed they were kitted up and on one hour alert in case they were to be shipped out to the Fauklands. If the military action had continued for only one more week, the British would have requested Australia's assistance. Through all these campaigns the Diggers perpetuated the myth of being great drinkers and tough fighters, on an off the battlefields, above and beyond what any other country could produce.

GROWTH IN THE TWENTIETH CENTURY

As Australia developed into a great agricultural nation, support industries grew up to serve this growing society. Wheat and wool made Australia an international economic force in agriculture by the end of the nineteenth century. Indeed, one of the favorite sayings was that 'Australia rides on the sheep's back', economically speaking. Like most other British colonies Australia's agricultural abundance was a cheap source of food and raw materials for Britain.

Even though many Australian manufacturing industries flourished in support of this thriving economy, the government influence in and regulation of the business community effectively shaped and severely retarded the future of Australian business. Australian business has been fighting a losing battle with government regulation, government competition and high taxation since the earliest of times.

From day one in Australia's development, the government and people have been hand–in–hand and almost totally dependent on each other. The prevailing attitude was and still is, "Give it a fair go (try), if it doesn't work the government will help me."

If a manufacturing business was having a difficult time competing with foreign based manufacturers, the government was only too happy to oblige with the institution of a protective tariff. Today the government is still involved with just about every aspect of life and business. So rather than experiencing the unfettered but watchdogged growth that the United States has enjoyed, Australia has reached only a fraction of the potential than would have been possible under a democratic, free enterprise republic system such as exists in the U.S. British thinking, methods and influences permeate the very infrastructure of Australian society, possibly crippling it beyond repair, perhaps leaving it too weakened to effectively face the challenges of the 1990's and the twenty-first century. Australia is in reality more of a socialist country than the free enterprise democracy it is purported to be. More about this subject in Chapter 5. (See Figure 5)

THE PEOPLE OF AUSTRALIA

Australia's population is derived from three basic sources. One third are the descendants of convicts, settlers and military personnel who arrived in the late 18th and early 19th centuries. These are the people who created the folklore and the pioneering legacy of Australian society. This legacy still runs deep in many aspects of contemporary Australian life.

Another third of the Australian population is composed of more recent immigrants from Britain. Still afflicted with their native accents, these recent (two or three generations is still considered recent in Australia) arrivals have been unaffectionately dubbed 'Pommies' or 'Poms'. These people opted to flee the limited horizons of a decaying British society to seek a better future for themselves and their children in Australia. Basic dreams of owning one's own home, only a wild dream to many Britons, often became a reality for these people soon after arriving in Australia.

The remaining roughly one third of the population has its origins in the towns and villages of Southern Europe. Australia is home to some of the largest Italian and Greek communities in the world. Most of these immigrants came to Australia after the Second World War during the post war industrial boom. 'Factory Fodder' was a less than courteous term used to describe this large influx of non-English speaking minorities into Australia. (See Figure 6)

One might think that Australia's development and its immigration history is very similar to that of the U.S.. There is one major difference. Except for the early free settlers and those wealthy families who ventured into the new world of young Australia, the vast majority of 20th century immigrants came to Australia on 'assisted passages'. This rather creative system is simply another way of saying the British and Australian governments subsidized millions of people as an inducement to go to Australia. There was a time when all one had to do was raise ten pounds (A$20) and one could buy his way to Australia with his immediate family. It could be argued quite strongly that when a nation has to bribe people to immigrate, as in Australia's case, the basic quality of people might be different from those who have to pay their own way to take advantage of the opportunities that await them in a new land. Of course this a generalization and there are always exceptions to any theory put forward as such, most notably the industriousness of many of the Southern Europeans in comparison to the British immigrant.

The character of each of these basic groups of immigrants was very different even though each was dedicated to the same goal of pioneering and developing their new land. The 'pioneering'

Intolerable
tolerance

from G. Mora

I read in your paper Professor Blainey's article (20/3) in which he states that Australians are now by far more tolerant to immigration than in 1950.

I am disturbed; I believed we immigrants were really wanted, not just "tolerated". I always thought that my new home, Australia, was a country in formation and development, which needed every man and woman who came here.

I also wonder who exactly has tolerance for whom? I arrived here 33 years ago. Am I now entitled to tolerate or not to tolerate the new arrivals? Or should I be happy to be accepted by those who arrived a hundred years ago?

If showing tolerance or intolerance to newcomers is the status of being a true Australian, I would rather step aside and remain a New Australian.

GEORGE MORA,
South Yarra.

Fig 6
(Courtesy of The Melbourne Age)

Constable Paul Wong is congrat-
ulated by his mother, Mrs Patri-
cia Wong, after graduating
yesterday as the first person of
Asian descent to join the Victoria Police Force.

Fig 7
(Courtesy of The Melbourne Age)

Australians have always been independent thinking and progressive activists in all aspects of Australian life when it comes to working for the removal of British control over Australia. The British immigrants on the other hand presented a stumbling block to this endeavor. Even though they had left their homeland for greener pastures, the British monarch was their Monarch of Australia and it was nothing short of anarchy to think of declaring independence from the British Commonwealth.

I have often pondered the question of whether there was a major conspiracy by British and Australian monarchists, entrenched at the controls of Australian society, whereby they planned to fill up Australia with loyal Britons so as to assure Australian loyalty to Britain for all time. What could hamper the move towards independence more than having a large portion of the population remain loyal monarchists?

Another social impact of the British immigrant is his influence on the Australian trade union movement. Trade unions were well established in Australia and seen by the average worker as a way to overcome the inherent injustices in young British ruled Australia. (It is an irony that Britain transported the Toll Puddle Martyrs, the first trade unionists, to Australia as a penalty for their activities.) Unfortunately for Australia, many of the British immigrants were themselves members of trade unions and became extremely active in the same field after they arrived in Australia. British trade unions have always been more militant and bone headed than their Australian counterparts, and this influence has helped lead to a virtual state of war between the worker and the employer in many Australian industries. The 'Pommie' shop steward is a well known fixture in many trade unions.

Australia's domination by Britain and large number of British immigrants brought with it the concept of social class that has crippled Britain for centuries. While there exists a large middle class similar to that in the U.S., Australia has its fair share of Lords and Ladies, titles conferred by the British Crown for services to the mother land. This also seems to be a very successful way to make the population conscious of the 'class factor' in everyday life. Trade unions also have much to gain by perpetuating this class consciousness. The working people of Australia once considered, and still do in many cases, trade unions as weapons against those with wealth. In contrast to this in most instances, the U.S. has come to terms with the employer/employee relationship and consider the trade unions, in conjunction with the law, as a legitimate means of working in the best interests of all concerned. Australian trade unions are often used to protect jobs regardless of the economic consequences to the industry and overall economy. More about this in Chapter 4.

The Southern Europeans, or 'Wogs' as they are insultingly called, displayed the usual characteristics of non-English speaking communities in English speaking countries. They collected in closely knit communities and worked very hard to support their families and fellow countrymen at every opportunity. Many of the older immigrants never learned more than a passing amount of English, enough to see them into menial jobs, many of which native born Australians and Britons were too proud to take. There were of course those maverick Southern Europeans who knew that if they wanted to participate more fully in the life of their newly adopted land, they would have to get involved. They learned the language, worked two or more jobs and moved into suburban neighborhoods, often doing far better than their native born Australian and British neighbors. There was and still is resentment to this type of hard work because it makes the average Australian and Englishman look lazy.

I believe that this basic mix of immigrant cultures in Australia has been responsible for the lack of forward thinking and constructive progress in achieving independence and great industrial strength. The forward thinking, independent-minded Australians are outnumbered two to one by traditional thinking Britons and 'don't make waves' Southern Europeans. Australia has a history of not voting for constitutional or social change. I believe that this is mainly a result of the 'assisted passage' immigrants and their origins.

Where are the Blacks and Asians, one might ask? The Australian government, up until the early 1970's, had an immigration policy known unofficially as 'The White Australia Policy'. While held in high regard by those bigots who base a country's character on the color of its inhabitant's skin, this policy was devised solely to prevent immigration by anyone other than persons of European origin.

Asians are represented in Australia by three main groups. The oldest group of Asian descent are the Chinese communities. In the Australian gold rush days of the 1850's, a large influx of Chinese was met with alarm by both the miners and the government. The state of Victoria actually banned Chinese immigration in 1856. As happened with the Chinese who came to the U.S. to work on the railways in the west, many stayed in Australia after the gold had run out and turned their hand to market gardening and other trades.

The second oldest group, but by far the smallest in number are exchange students from Australia's S.E. Asian neighbors to the north. Many of these students marry Australians and take up residence in Australia.

The most recent group of Asians, and the most controversial to come to Australia, are the Vietnamese. In the past three or four years, Australia has taken the largest number of Vietnamese refugees second only to the U.S.

The recent influx of Vietnamese refugees, in times of high unemployment and economic recession, has been the cause of increasing racial hatred in some Australian communities. Seen as getting unlimited government assistance, anti-Vietnamese sentiment has revived a call for the re-institution of the white Australia policies of the past. Fear of 'the Asian hoards' overtaking Australia has been used for decades as a conservative tactic in Australian politics. The idea of Asian and Black immigrants raised the spectre in some minds of polluting the white race of Australia. (See Figures 7, 8 & 9)

When the subject of America's Black history is raised, Australians are also quick to forget that they had their own slave trade in the north. Pacific Islanders were 'black birded' into cutting sugarcane for plantation owners. Black races in Australia are represented by the Aborigines. Only 1.1% of the Australian population is made up of Aborigines. Just as parts of America are known as the 'Deep South' due to their past and present attitudes to blacks and life in general, so too is Queensland known as the 'Deep North' of Australia.

New Zealanders comprise another rapidly growing minority in Australia. New Zealand is in such economic turmoil that one percent of her population per year has migrated across the Tasman Sea to Australia's shores in recent years. New Zealanders cause a degree of discomfort to the Australian way of life as they have the highest crime rate of any ethnic minority in Australia. This growing tide will

KIDS' STUFF

In a corner of the playground a bunch of them are at it again, playing the school's oldest game: baiting the new kid.

This should be an extra good game; Nguyen is so different from any of them. But the kid doesn't know the rules. He doesn't panic or cringe, he's quick on his feet, and he can use his hands.

Why do they play the game? It's not so long since Bruno and Ioannis and Mahomet were new kids themselves; even Wayne and Kevin were new kids once. Have they forgotten what it's like?

They remember only too well. But the rules of the game are, you don't try getting back at the older kids, you take it out on the next lot. New kid! New kid! New kid!

Fig 8
(Courtesy of The Melbourne Age)

Only 8000 Indo-Chinese refugees this year

The Federal Government plans to reduce the number of refugees coming from Indo-China. On preliminary estimates, only 8000 Indo-Chinese will be offered places in Australia this financial year.

Fig 9
(Courtesy of The Melbourne Age)

not be halted as there are few restrictions on travel between the two countries.

As in the United States, you can find people from almost every nation in Australia. They are there for various reasons, but it is clear that most of the permanent immigrants are there because the conditions are better in Australia than in the immigrants original homeland.

Consider for a moment why Americans do not make up any significant portion of the Australian population. Only .2% of the Australian population was born in the U.S. The answer might be that Australia does not have very much to offer the average American outside of a good time on vacation.

The lifestyle in Australia's towns and suburbs, where about 84% of the population live, is very similar to that of the average Californian. Most Australians strive to buy a home if they can afford it, they drive Ford and GM's, they eat McDonalds and Kentucky Fried fast food. Most people work Monday to Friday and have week-ends off. They watch T.V. with a goodly smattering of American shows and plenty of homegrown sport on the week-ends. Their children play on their own sports teams. There are beaches, mountains, forests and deserts to explore, and there are plenty of city cultural activities to enjoy. In fact, it may all sound a little too similar to the U.S. It is this similarity, when only viewed on the surface, that has led millions of Americans to believe Australia must be a better place to live. A continent the same size as the continental United States, with the same lifestyle and only 16 million people, should be better place to live. Unfortunately, when the surface similarities are stripped away, vast differences become apparent that will have a great effect on the average American's view of Australia.(See Figure 10)

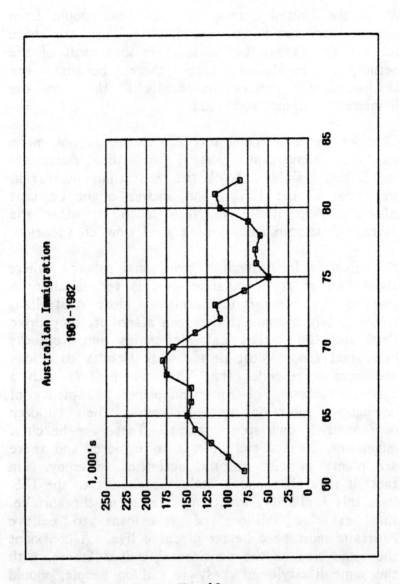

Fig 10

Chapter Three

Answers
to
the
Most
Commonly
Asked
Questions
About
Australia

The following questions are taken from the myriad of questions in their different forms that have been asked of me since 1981. These particular fifteen questions represent those most commonly asked.

#1 I'VE HEARD THERE'S LOTS OF WOMEN IN AUSTRALIA?

Unlike most ex–colonies that were perceived to have an excess of males, Australia is supposed to be some kind of writhing mass of single women waiting to devour any stray foreign male fortunate enough to make it to her shores. It seems that the great receptions given U.S. military personnel upon their arrival in Australian ports contributed to this modern day fable. The ratio of women to men is close to 1:1 in Australia.

#2 YOU DON'T HAVE BIG CITIES IN AUSTRALIA DO YOU?

The image of sparsely populated wide open spaces still has some truth in it today as there are only 16 million people inhabiting roughly the same area as the continental United States. The average population density is low but the major cities are big. Sydney, Australia's largest metropolitan area, boasts 3.3 million people while the second largest metropolitan area, Melbourne, has 2.9 million people. These two cities account for almost half the entire population of Australia. (See Figures 11 & 12)

#3 AREN'T THERE PLENTY OF JOBS IN AUSTRALIA?

The answer is a resounding NO! The Australian job market in the last ten years has been as bad or worse than it is here in the U.S. Australian unemployment is currently higher than that of the U.S. and what jobs there are usually pay less than here. The scope of Australian jobs for long term pay and promotional opportunities is much more limited than Americans are used to finding. The basis for this big question seems to come from a few decades ago when there were programs offered by the Australian government in an attempt to attract skilled labor to that country. My wife Bonnie participated in one of these programs that recruited school teachers during the 1960's and 1970's. (See Figures 13 & 14)

#4   I'VE HEARD THAT THE WEATHER IS GREAT DOWN UNDER?

Unless you live in Perth, in Western Australia, where the climate is very similar to that in San Diego, California, or live inland in the eastern states, there are few areas that can claim to have good weather, especially by Californian standards. I am not under the delusion that the entire U.S. has weather like California mind you. True, there are no major population areas that have to endure long winter periods of snow and sub-zero temperatures, but Melbourne has rain an average of 140 days per year, it's often $100^{\circ}F+$ there during the summer with high humidity, then it's cold with overcast skies or driving rains during the winter. A travel article in a local Sacramento newspaper once described Melbourne's weather as mild! Look at Sydney, Australia's largest city. It is a sub-tropical sweat box complete with torrential downpours during high humidity summers consoled only by mild winters. (See Figure 15)

#5   YOU DON'T PAY MUCH TAX IN AUSTRALIA DO YOU?

This question makes me cry. It has even been suggested on more than a few occasions that Australians don't pay any taxes!!!!!! Income taxes

To minimise air pollution risk, the EPA advises that outdoor fires and incinerators should not be lit and, where possible, cars should not be used.

Fig 11
(Courtesy of The Melbourne Age)

Air to breathe around us

THE NEED for a better life support system got a bit of a nudge this week with an observation by a visiting air pollution expert from Canada, Dr David Bates, professor of medicine and physiology at the University of British Columbia in Vancouver, that Melbourne's brown pall of photochemical smog may soon rival that over Los Angeles.

Fig 12
(Courtesy of The Melbourne Age)

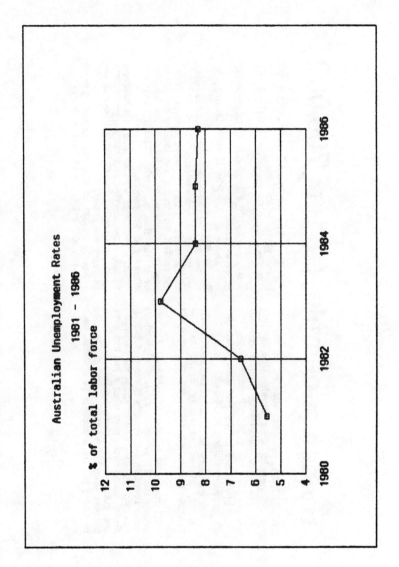

Fig 13

'Hidden' unemployed top 700,000

CANBERRA. — The number of unemployed people who would like a job but are not receiving unemployment benefits — the "hidden" unemployed — rose by 56,000 or 8.7 per cent over the six months ending in March.

This category of unemployed now totals 706,300, almost as many again as the 718,600 people officially out of work in May.

Of the total hidden unemployed 113,200 people (up 46 per cent on last September) were listed in yesterday's Bureau of Statistics survey as "discouraged job-seekers". These were people who want a job but have not taken active steps to look for work because they believe they would not be able to find a job for a number of reasons, such as:

● They are considered by employers to be too young or too old.
● They have language or racial difficulties.
● They lack the necessary training, skills or experience.
● There are no jobs in their locality, or line or work.

The bulk of these discouraged job-seekers, 96,000 were females.

The bureau's survey found that the highest ranked reason for not looking for a job was that there were no jobs in the locality or in the line of work. This reason was cited by 66,300 people.

Many of the discouraged job-seekers, 83,400, were married and the biggest single group, accounting for 27,200, fell in the 45-54-years age group.

Nearly 80,000 of the discouraged people had not had a job for at least a year.

Fig 14
(Courtesy of The Melbourne Age)

start at 25%, then rise quickly to reach 60% for amounts earned over $35,000 per year! This shows Australia is not a low tax country or no tax country by any stretch of the imagination. Combine these figures with sales taxes between 7%–32.5% and almost no tax deductions for the average working person, and Australia stands out as a high tax country compared to the U.S. (See Figure 16)

#6 I UNDERSTAND AUSTRALIA'S COST OF LIVING IS LOW?

There may have been a speck of truth in this at one time, but alas, the cost of living in Australia is much higher than the average cost of living in America. Jobs usually pay less than comparable jobs in the U.S. and incomes are taxed more heavily in Australia. The cost of a dozen eggs is around A$1.75, milk costs A$2.90 per gallon, gasoline costs A$1.85 per gallon. Homes cost more with less amenities and mortgage interest rates are currently 15% and not tax deductible. (See Figure 17)

#7 ISN'T THE PACE OF LIFE SLOWER IN AUSTRALIA?

America's fast pace of life, so to speak, is conjured up by outsiders viewing downtown New York and Los Angeles. Similarly, Australia's mythical slow pace of life is based on the life style in the remote out of the way places few people live. Generally speaking, based on having lived in Melbourne and in the San Francisco Bay Area, visiting New York City, Philadelphia and Los Angeles, the pace of life for the average suburbanite in Australia is much faster than for the average American suburbanite. I am defining the pace of life as the speed at which you have to juggle work, personal and family life, your hobbies and entertainment. As most all stores in Australia up until this writing close at 5.30pm M–F and 1pm

Saturdays, the strategic plans required to accomplish shopping for food, clothing and household needs are daunting. If you are an average family where both partners work full-time jobs, then most of your shopping time is packed into before 5:30pm and one or two nights till 9pm during the week, or before 1pm on Saturdays. It is like Christmas crowds all year round.

#8   AREN'T AUSTRALIAN DRIVERS BETTER THAN OURS?

A recent study by an Australian university found that Australian drivers were the most aggressive road users in the world. They generally drive too fast, too close and without regard to other road users. It is very common to be forced to stop on a freeway on-ramp because those motorists on the freeway will not open up a space for you to enter. Australian drivers once held the infamous glory of being among the most drunken of all. This problem became so intolerable that the drunken driving laws were changed a few years back and are now some of the toughest in the world. The penalties for having as little as .05% blood alcohol level include mandatory jail sentences, fines and license cancellations. The introduction of these tough drunk driving penalties and the mandatory use of seat belts for all vehicle occupants has produced a commendable drop in motor vehicle accident injuries and deaths. The U.S. could take a leaf out of Australia's book on this one. (See Figure 18)

#9   DOES EVERYONE SPEAK ENGLISH?

In a manner of speaking, yes! The Australian language is far removed from everyday British and American English. It has been so changed for everyday use that it can often be almost unintelligable by other English speaking peoples. The

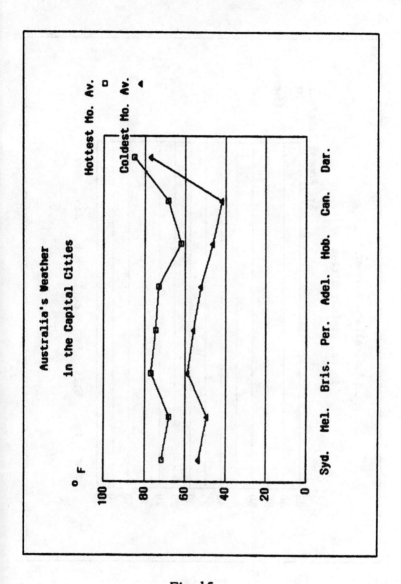

Fig 15a

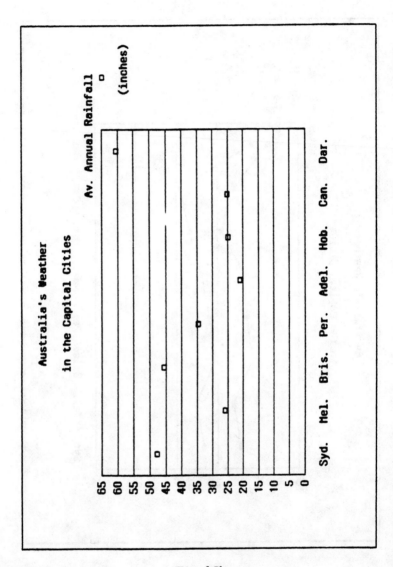

Fig 15b

How tax man takes his cut

THE personal income tax scale from November 1

Taxable income $	Tax payable
0 to 4595	Nil
4596 to 12,500	Nil plus 25c for each $1 in excess of $4595.
12,501 to 19,500	$1976.25 plus 30c for each $1 in excess of $12,500.
19,501 to 28,000	$4076.25 plus 46c for each $1 in excess of $19,500.
28,001 to 35,000	$7986.25 plus 48c for each $1 in excess of $28,000.
35,001 and over	$11,346.25 plus 60c for each $1 in excess of $35,000.

Fig 16
(Courtesy of The Melbourne Age)

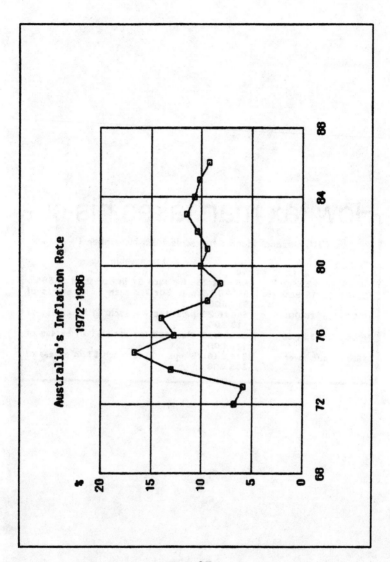

Fig 17

toilet can be called "the dunny" (crude term) or "the loo"; a ball point pen is called "a biro"; the hood of a car "the bonnet" and the trunk is called "the boot". The fender is "the mudguard" and the mudguard is "the mudflap". When you are "pissed" you are drunk and when you open a can of beer you "crack a tube". The pub can be called "the rubuddy dub" and gays are called "poofters". A car accident can be called a "prang" and to "nick-off" is to run away. "Gedday" means hello and "ooroo" can be used for good-bye. If someone says it's your "shout" then you buy the next round of drinks at the bar. There have been many books written about the Australian language and they all try to put it in some kind of logical perspective, trying to relate different Australian accents to different geographic regions. The debate will go on indefinitely but I do not believe an Australian can be identified by his accent or manner of speech beyond a cursory observation of the person being from the city or the bush. Unfortunately for the English language, the slang or colloquialisms are used daily by all kinds of people including the mass media.

#10   ARE THERE REALLY KANGAROOS AND KOALAS EVERYWHERE?

These unique and best known of all Australian animals are Australia's international trademarks. They are rather common, but you don't find them roaming around the suburbs. It is KOALA, not Koala Bear as most Americans say. If you want to make an Australian angry just keep saying Koala Bear all the time. These cuddly little animals are not related to the bear family. The koala is protected by wildlife laws and tends not to cause anyone any grief. Although there are reported cases of koalas being killed, their future seems assured as long as their bush environment stays intact. Australians have a lousy tradition of "If it moves, shoot it; If it doesn't move, chop it down!" The kangaroo is very widespread but is still slaughtered by the millions each year to placate the powerful Australian ranching lobby. Kangaroos compete very efficiently with sheep and cattle for grazing land. The most common place that Australians see kangaroos is in their dog and cat food! The Red Kangaroo was near extinction a decade ago, and the government placed a ban on the export of kangaroo products. This ban has been lifted recently prompting the kangaroo products industry to search for new markets for skins and meat products. Kangaroo meat is of the highest quality and apparently the Germans have developed quite a taste for kangaroo meat this past year. The vast majority of Australians have never eaten kangaroo meat, nor would they ever have the opportunity to do so.

11. DO YOU PAY MUCH FOR CARS AND GAS IN AUSTRALIA?

You bet we do. The basic reason for this is that by law 80% of all new cars sold must be built in Australia. Therefore, the import tariffs and duties on imported cars are so high that the prices of domestic cars reflect these inflated import prices rather than the cost of building cars in Australia. Australians pay about 15%-30% more for autos than Americans. Also keep in mind that interest on a vehicle loan is not tax deductible; when buying a car on terms, and who doesn't these days, the cost of a car in Australia is about 30%-50% higher than in the U.S. Gas is a very pricey item in Australia also. Like the U.S., Australia produces a large amount of its own oil, 70%-80% of its requirements. The price of oil is determined however by the price Saudi Arabia charges. That's right, the government one day said that the oil producers could charge Saudi prices on all old oil and new oil as an incentive for exploration. The price is kept even higher because of the outrageous amounts of federal and state taxes, more than half the cost at the gas pump! At 56 cents per liter compared to about 26–30 cents per liter here in Northern California, gas is very expensive. Australia introduced unleaded gas in 1986 and it is expected prices will rise even further.

12. ARE THERE ANY COLORED PEOPLE IN AUSTRALIA?

A commonly asked question by white folks. (The term 'colored' is the most common word used when people ask about the black population of Australia. In real terms it could be interpreted to mean anyone of non-white race.) Not many! The Aborigines as described in the second chapter are the only real 'blacks' in Australia. The 'White Australia' immigration policies kept all colored races out of Australia with the exception of Indians and the Ceylonese, as India and Ceylon were members of the British Commonwealth. Asians, previous to the recent flood of Vietnamese refugees, could enter Australia only to attend college. Much of the anti-black sentiment in Australia is helped along by the British immigrant sector of the Australian population and the arch conservative northerners.

13. IF YOU'RE FROM AUSTRALIA HOW COME YOU'RE WHITE AND SPEAK ENGLISH?

I included this choice question because it does indicate that there are some Americans who know only of Australia's primitive history. It was actually asked by a mid-westerner acquaintance of ours. It is amazing in this day of advanced communications that someone could have only been exposed to the Aboriginal culture of Australia. It may not be too surprising however when people still ask, "where is Australia anyway?". Australia is quite often mistaken by people who think one is talking about Austria.

14. HAVEN'T YOU GOT SOCIALIZED MEDICINE IN AUSTRALIA?

In 1973 a system was introduced by the federal Labor government that allowed an individual to attend his regular doctor, specialists, hospitals etc. and receive 85% of the cost of those services refunded to him, or his physician could bill the government directly and the patient paid nothing, directly. One year later, in 1974, the system was cost analyzed and then on his tax return all taxpayers paid a small levy, less than $150 per year depending on his marital status and number of dependents. Alas, this world beater national health system was destroyed by subsequent governments.

15. THE SCHOOLS ARE MUCH BETTER THAN OURS AREN'T THEY?

The U.S. has a basically undeserving inferiority complex about its educational system. It would seem there are as many private schools in Australia as there are public ones. This is because the federal government actually gives money directly to private schools, often at a higher rate than to the state government operated schools! That's right, the Australian taxpayer actually helps those more wealthy than himself give the wealthy children a better education than his own children. Most charitable of the average working Australian. Many of these private schools are church run and government support is even in spite of a constitutional ban on assistance to churches. So the government schools cry out for more resources while the government gives money to already wealthy schools. Each state controls its public schools, both in the cities and the counties. My wife Bonnie's elementary teaching experience indicated that elementary schools in Victoria were marginally superior to those in California from an academic stand point. In contrast to this, most

Australian public high schools are academically oriented, lacking in many of the social, musical, club and other important social growth activities that are commonly found in American public high schools. Drug use is on the rise in many Australian schools, as is student violence against teachers. A principal told us recently that four teachers at a neighboring elementary school had been injured in the six months prior to our visit. Corporal punishment has been recently banned in Victorian state schools. Class size varies depending on where one is and the amount of political clout the school district can muster. Thirty children per class is common and the teaching quality varies as much as it does in the U.S. Australia is also trying to gear education more towards the business needs of the future similar to the educational movement in the U.S.

Melbourne drivers aggressive: university study

ANYONE who has tried Melbourne traffic at peak hour on a hot day would have little trouble agreeing with the latest finding of a Melbourne University team that Melbourne drivers are the most aggressive.

Seeking a fuel economy test to replace the present AS2077 cycle, the Melbourne University team under Dr Harry Watson and Eric Milkins found an American-based test inadequate because of our driving habits.

Fig 18
(Courtesy of The Melbourne Age)

Chapter Four

Working In Australia

HOW HARD DO AUSTRALIANS REALLY WORK?

It has been said that Australians work only at one pace - SLOWLY! While this is a generalization, there is substantially more than a grain of truth in it. An appropriate analogy of the pace Australians work at is: Englishmen work twice as hard as Irishmen; Australians work twice as hard as Englishmen; Americans work twice as hard as Australians, and the Japanese work twice as hard as everyone else put together!

Most Americans would find the work pace much slower if they moved to Australia and worked in an Australian operated business. Generally, the only Australians who work as hard as their U.S. counterparts, are the self employed, and there are even exceptions to this. An acquaintance of ours who owns and operates an independent meat market expressed his right not be penalized by competition from supermarkets because he wanted to work only a 40 hour week! He felt that the supermarkets had no right to sell meat when his store wasn't open for business!!!!. These Australians to a large extent face the stiff competition of the market place, and are not protected by Government agencies nor regulated by the mindless self-defeating power of the Australian trade unions.

When on a job site that is controlled by a trade union in Australia, everyone works about as slowly as the least productive person to ensure that no one looks bad. Many times I was personally chastised and told to slacken my work pace, because I would make others appear lazy. Rarely is there any consideration for your own pride in workmanship or efficiency. To work hard, smart and fast in a union controlled environment is akin to a declaration of war on your work mates. The more productive worker is not only subjected to verbal inuendoes and smart-alec cracks, but in extreme cases he might be subjected to bodily injury by his disgruntled union coworkers. To keep the peace Australian workers kowtow to the status quo and sluff off, working at a pace that would seem like "siesta time" to most Americans.

Some American workers may say "it's not a bad idea, America is a far too competitive place anyway and it would do the nation good to take a leaf out of Australia's book and slow down and take it easy". I hope that these workers realize the consequences of such a worker attitude. Australia and Great Britain are living examples of a lazy work force protected by mindless unionism and bloated government budgets. The result is a drab, go-nowhere place that produces a self-fulfilling miserable prophecy when it comes to the crunch. Lazy workers equal low productivity, low wages, less job opportunities, higher taxes, and less affluence for everyone. Plenty for workers to stand around and complain about. Some readers might say "all that is not such a bad idea anyway. Americans could use a dose of less affluence to make them really realize what they have". That may be so, but Australia is an example of a country where brilliant people are born and raised, but the society does not let them soar with eagles, only taxi with turkeys! Many Australians leave Australia to more fully develop their careers overseas. Great success in Australia is not easily come by unless you are born wealthy or study/work overseas for a time. Then one can learn how to beat the Australian economic and social systems.

WHO DO AUSTRALIANS WORK FOR?

Like the United States, Australia is a pluralistic, twentieth century industrialized society. Australians perform the same types of jobs as Americans. Our circle of Australian friends and acquaintances did consist of large numbers of school teachers, nurses and bank clerks. This small sample of Australian workers reflects the biggest difference between who Australians and Americans work for.

Americans are apt to scream bloody murder at the thought of the federal, state and local governments employing 12% of the national work force. Australians are living with a government workforce approaching 30% of the nation's employed. Sound somewhat like a socialist country? The Australian government workforces also consist of employees of the phone company, the power companies, the water companies, the railways, the one international airline, one major internal airline, most of the banks and on and on and on. Most all government and government independent body jobs are very secure. With few exceptions, a worker would have to murder his supervisor before being fired from his job. While job security is a highly valued benefit for any worker, almost unbreakable security regardless of the worker's ability to do the job is down right stupidity. This kind of security breeds generation after generation of lazy, inefficient public servants, sucking up vast amounts of tax revenues produced by the sweat of many relatively hard-working Australians.

TRADE UNIONS AND THEIR ROLE/EFFECT.

The reader may have gathered from the first section of this chapter that my attitude towards the Australian Trade Union movement is somewhat negative. I came from a good working class, pro-union background and I always belonged to unions in my workplace. This seemed fine and appropriate to me at the time because of the "state of war" that exists between most Australian employees and their employers. This undeclared war, where both sides try to screw as much out of the other without regard to the consequences, is a legacy of the myopic British way of doing things. Traditionally in Britain, as in early U.S. industrialization, the employers were members of the wealthy ruling class and the employees were from the poorer classes put on earth for the use of those who knew better and had a god-given right to rule their social and economic inferiors. There was seldom a great desire or opportunity for any of the employees to rise out of the masses and create their own wealth and thus transcend the classes to join the employers. Unlike America, where many of the "small people" see no wrong in wanting to achieve greatness and wealth far above what they were born to, Australians on the whole say that they are more than happy with their lot and have little desire to tackle greater challenges. The Australian Trade Union movement shares much of the blame for this socially and economically numbing state of affairs.

There has been federal regulation of trade unions for many years, but there are no union contracts as Americans know them. When a dispute arises, and they often do, if the union representative and employer cannot work it out then alternative procedures are sought. Depending on past relationships between the two sides, such alternative action may result in wildcat strike action, which it very often does. The terms of employment between an employer and his employees are set by federal 'awards'. These 'awards' set out all the conditions of employment in each different industry which employers must honor. There is no signed and sealed legally binding agreement between any parties in the industrial arena that can be subjected to quick court hearings if either party breaches the agreement. (See Figure 19)

Without quick resolution of the tremendous numbers of wildcat strikes, it is easy to see why Australia loses more work days due to industrial disputes than there are union members in most years. Almost two

The Accord has been at work in Australia for over a year.

It shows that the government and the unions can work together and through everyone's co-operation, outstanding benefits are being achieved for all Australians.

Over 258,000 new jobs have been created. Unemployment has been reduced. Inflation has been almost halved, bringing it down to the lowest level for more than a decade.

Industrial harmony has given Australia its lowest rate of industrial disputation for 16 years.

Strong economic recovery has placed Australia at the head of western countries in anticipated economic growth for 1984.

And working people have received wage increases of 8.6% to protect their incomes against inflation.

These dramatic results have only been achieved by everybody playing their part in The Accord. But let's not forget there is a long way to go.

The continued success of The Accord, with its obvious and increasing benefits for all Australians, is dependent on everyone's commitment to the spirit of co-operation.

Keep to The Accord, play your part to the full, and together we'll build a better Australia.

AUSTRALIA
AUSTRALIAN GOVERNMENT

THE ACCORD.
BUILDING A BETTER AUSTRALIA.

Fig 19
(Courtesy of The Melbourne Age)

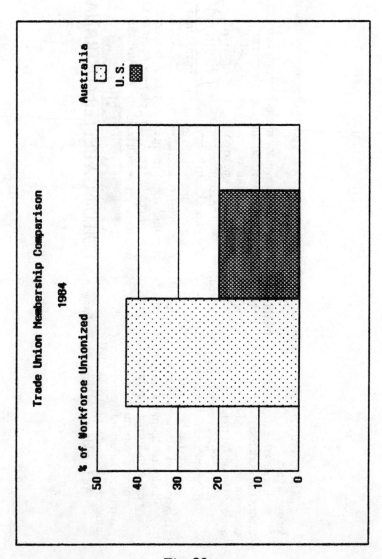

Fig 20a

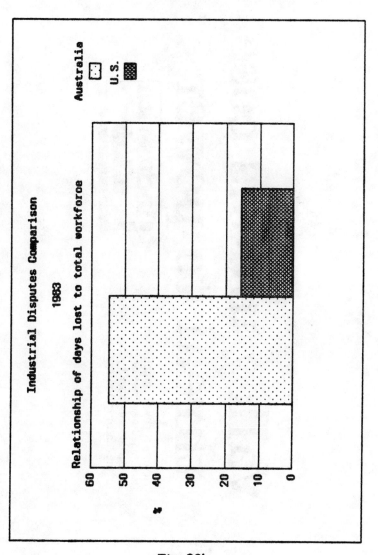

Fig 20b

Valley unions pose threat to power

Industrial affairs

Victoria's power supplies could be threatened next week because of an industrial campaign by nine unions in the Latrobe Valley.

Fig 21
(Courtesy of The Melbourne Age)

thirds of Australia's workforce is unionised but there is more than one day of work per year lost in industrial disputes for every union member. So, unlike the U.S., where union/employer contracts are protection for both sides, trying to ensure a stable and profitable ongoing relationship, in Australia this situation is so uncontrolled that it ensures continued disruption in the workplace regardless of the economic consequences. (See Figure 20)

Let me relate a number of labor disputes to illustrate my point. There is a fabled dispute, often quoted in conversation that cites a factory dispute of the highest stupidity. An employer decided one day to buy a diffent brand of cookie for the workers' morning and afternoon breaks. The problem arose as this is such an earth shattering decision it should not have been made without the assistance of the union representative. The type of cookie the workers eat strikes at the very heart of industrial relations. When the union members discovered this covert cookie operation, they immediately notified their union representative. In a matter of hours the situation reached such heated proportions that all factory union members were called out on a wildcat strike. Before the end of the work day, after much heavy duty bargaining, the problem was resolved when the employer relented and sent the office helper down to the local supermarket to reinstate the favorite cookie brand. The wildcat strike was called off and work returned to normal. Fable or fact, it is not at all unreasonable that such an event could take place in the Australian work environment. (See Figure 21)

The following real-life example of trade union thinking, Australian style, is from the 1983/84 files. The Victorian state railway system is served by numerous unions covering various job descriptions all with their own individual 'awards'. It so happens that locomotive engineers and railway electricians belong to different unions. These personnel work for a state wide passenger and freight system serving millions of taxpayers daily. It is not illegal for government workers to strike. There is a rule in railway cafeterias that any uniformed employees should be served their meals before non-uniformed employees. The simple and logical reason for this is that uniformed employees are engineers, guards, station attendants etc., all of whom have very tight schedules that keep this massive public utility running on time, if at all possible. It so happens that the other non-uniformed employees, of which electricians are a part, have less rigorous schedules and can accommodate changes in their daily time schedule.

One day in the main Melbourne railway cafeteria, an electrician was in line to be served lunch when the cashier asked a uniformed engineer to step forward to be served first. Apparently something clicked inside the electrician's head and he protested this action which gave privileges to a member of a particular union. Various verbal unpleasantries followed between all concerned. Suddenly the electrician took the unprecedented step of turning off the power to the cafeteria! This catapaulted a stupid unfriendly encounter into a state-wide industrial dispute affecting literally millions of citizens.

In response to the electrical shut down of the eating facility, the engineers' and guards' union called upon all members to stop working because they could no longer get food at their work location. This stoppage soon spread to other locations throughout the state and then the electricians union, in response to the train stoppage, shut off all power to the entire state rail system! This brief lunchtime encounter had turned into an outright industrial breakdown. The next step was a railways management mediator stepping in to try and clean up this mess. You note I have not mentioned if management tried to stop the shutdowns etc., simply because they were never in control of the situation to begin with. The unions could take this and any other actions as they wished. With much ado they came to some understanding between unions and the system was restored to operation after leaving some million or so commuters stranded to seek alternative transportation home that evening rush hour.

This is a normal account of the kind of problems that confront Australian industrial relations in this day and age. (See Figure 22)

Another account of belligerent short-sighted unionism is shown in the battles between The Builders Laborers Federation and the now defunct construction company known as Mainline. These confrontations took place in downtown Melbourne in the 1970's, where large scale construction of highrise towers was in progress.

The Builders Laborers Federation membership performed basic jobs on construction sites like pouring concrete foundations. For many years the union and the Mainline company contested many issues regarding their job sites. The secretary of the union, who is the most powerful of all union officials, (who is now in jail for accepting kick-backs and the union is deregistered) happened to take a great dislike to the management of this construction company, so he decided the union should press for some claims outside and in excess of the current 'award'.

The plan of attack was to call wildcat strikes to disrupt the workplace and curtail the profits of Mainline. As all construction people know there are many weak spots in the construction steps of a building and one of these is the pouring of foundations. The concrete for steel reinforced foundations must be a continuous operation from start to finish. The secretary of the union seized on this opportunity and called what seemed to be endless wildcat strikes during the foundation pours on many building sites. These wildcat strikes would last only long enough to allow the concrete to set before the laborers returned to work. Needless to say the first job when they returned to work was to dig out the recently hardened concrete and prepare for another attempt at completing the foundations.

This situation went on for months and only affected the Mainline construction company. Soon there ensued a press battle between the company and the union. The company claimed the union actions amounted to extortion and the union claimed the company could easily give in to the increased pay and benefits demands because the company was so wealthy. The red flag went out one day when the company insisted it would go bankrupt if the interruptions to foundation pours continued. Regardless of these warnings the union and its members, in good lemming fashion, continued their suicidal efforts to put pressure on the company. Finally the crunch came. Mainline went bankrupt and put some 2000 Builders Laborers Federation members out of work! Poetic justice to say the least. But to add insult to injury, the union screamed bloody murder and demanded that the company pay them for their lost time and for being put out of a job! The union secretary's attitude after this major industrial upheaval was, "Well they weren't a good company to work for anyway". Jail and deregistering of his union sure took care of his attitude problem in 1986.

Where was the government all this time? Nowhere to be seen because they have no power in the work place nor do the courts for that matter when it comes down to it. Everyone just shrugged it off as another lousy big company screwing over its workers because they didn't want to give them a pay raise. (See Figure 23)

Employers blast State's labor relations

One of Victoria's biggest employer groups yesterday strongly attacked the State Government's industrial relations performance, describing aspects of it as incompetent, belligerent and confused.

The criticism, from the Victorian Chamber of Manufactures, is the harshest since the Labor Government won office and indicates a growing level of employer disenchantment with the Government's industrial relations.

Another employer group, the Victorian Employers Federation, also accused the Government of being "locked in" to union demands, particularly over occupational health and safety laws.

The criticism follows a series of awkward and costly disputes involving the Government. The most recent are the MCG light towers dispute, which remains unresolved and which is estimated to have cost about $1.3 million in the use of police and delays to the job; and the nurses dispute which is unresolved after nine weeks despite a $7 million settlement proposed by the Government.

The Government was also forced yesterday to concede defeat on its plan to wrap all power industry unions in a single agreement, linking all movements in wages and conditions.

Most of the important blue collar unions rejected the approach and what could have been a milestone for the Government has now become just another millstone.

Fig 22
(Courtesy of The Melbourne Age)

Government plans to pay BLF strikers: Kennett

Tuesday 7 August 1984

The State Opposition yesterday claimed the Government would pay up to $300,000 to reimburse Builders' Laborers Federation workers on a Government project for time they lost during a recent four-week strike.

Fig 23
(Courtesy of The Melbourne Age)

Finally a personal experience with the power of Australian trade unions. I worked for the Victorian state railway system as a police officer or By-Laws Inspector as we were more commonly known.

One morning while patrolling suburban commuter trains with two fellow officers we picked up two juveniles for theft of railway property, to wit five shunter's lanterns, used in the freight yards at night while shunting freight cars. This theft of $300 worth of goods developed into a situation that nearly closed down the entire state rail system.

In the course of our investigations we were informed that a locomotive was missing for four hours the previous evening. Background checks confirmed that these same juveniles at one time had previously been caught inside running locomotives with the full knowledge and information of how to drive them. Being conscientious officers of the law, we saw this as an opportunity to pursue the suspects for a federal felony of illegal use of a locomotive.

Needless to say the best laid plans of mice and men don't always work out. While we were reinterviewing the suspects about the missing locomotive, word came down directly from our supervising sergeant that we were not to pursue the matter any further, and the sooner the juveniles were released the better for all concerned.

While we were attempting to build our case against the suspects, it had been confirmed that a night watchman, who happened to belong to our union, was asleep at his post and thus was unable to stop the youthful joyriders from stealing a multi-million dollar locomotive for the evening. Furthermore, if we were to charge the night watchman with neglect of duty the union would have no alternative but to call a state wide rail strike because one of its members was being harassed by his coworkers. The union's primary goal was to protect one of its members regardless of the fact that the watchman was derelict in his duty and public safety was at great risk! That is really where Australia's Trade Union movement's head is at. Amazingly, the decision to stop the inquiries was supported by rail management!

The scary part of the whole Australian labor/management situation is that it appears there is nobody willing to do anything constructive to come to grips with these entrenched problems. As soon as employers raise the issue, trade unions think they are being unfairly attacked. What is it like to live with this kind of free-for-all industrial relations? Every year around Christmas (summer holidays in Australia), the airlines, railways, postal workers, power companies and sundry others go on strike to pursue higher demands from their employers. These strikes inconvenience millions of law-abiding taxpayers who want to enjoy their vacations, to receive mail service and to have electricity supplied to their homes. Yet there is no penalty for these government workers or any others when they participate in wildcat strikes. There is almost no other type of strike but the wildcat.

Australian dock workers also have a worldwide notorious reputation for industrial disputes. In 1981/82, Australian dock workers lost more man hours in strikes than the rest of the world's ports put together! Not bad for a small country. In 83/84 there was some relief. Australian dock workers lost only the same number of days as the rest of the world's ports put together.

Trade unions paralyze the Australian economy. If one works in a union shop one has to join or be forced out. There is no such thing as an effective

48

"right to work" in Australia. These insane union activities give rise to increased costs for just about everything imaginable inside Australia. If Australia wants to get to the heart of its economic problems, reform of the trade union movement is one place to start. (See Figure 24)

MANAGEMENT IN AUSTRALIA

As it takes two to tango it is necessary to delve into management's way of thinking in the vast majority of Australian owned and operated businesses. One over-riding factor that guides most of Australian management is 'Don't Rock The Boat'. This stems from the fact that there is no court system or other method of back-up if management wants to take on the unions at their own game.

Any management operation that wants to circumvent the union system in the work place, must be able to creatively structure the company so the employees are well taken care of and offer possibilities for advancement through the ranks or in their own specialities. This may sound like an opening for imaginative American management. Many American companies are operating extremely well in Australia unthreatened by union actions or their possible influence in the company.

Unions tend to grow in response to unacceptable conditions imposed by an employer, unless they are an irrationally inseparable part of business as in Australia. It is also true that unions cannot take hold when a fresh approach is taken by management to address the needs of the workers. British management failure is quite evident when one looks at the miserable condition of Great Britain in comparison to the U.S. in the area of industrial relations. The same applies in Australia. Companies towing the old British management lines are the dinosaurs of the Australian economy, whereas the American upstarts that are highly capitalized and offer benefits, bonuses, medical insurance and other standard American fare, are the more progressive business concerns within Australia. Of course there are some well-heeled Australian businesses that very early recognized what American management had to offer and forged ahead of their sleepy Australian competitors a number of years ago and are still doing well today.

As Australia is owned to a large extent by the British, Americans and Japanese, it is probably only a matter of time until the traditional Australian trade union becomes an anacronism and makes a rational 20th century upgrade to serve the needs of its members and their country properly. Until that time, those upstart Americans and forward thinking Australian companies, will continue to make handsome inroads into the Australian industrial relations status-quo.

JOB ADVANCEMENT AND STABILITY

As mentioned earlier, if one works for somebody else one has to more or less await the demise of his supervisor before advancing to a higher level of responsibility within an Australian organization. As the vast number of Australian government and large corporate workers know, it is quite possible to stay in one job one's entire life, never get evaluated, get pay rises each year for service and inflation, then retire with not one earned promotion to show for it. The "Peter Principle" also works in Australia because all the incompetents are promoted to positions of inefficiency to get them out of people's hair and end up in redundant positions. Most Australians would suffer great anxiety if they had to live with the usual U.S. conditions of hard work and competition.

Employers hit repeal of 45 D

CANBERRA. — National employers yesterday reaffirmed their total opposition to the Federal Government's planned repeal of section 45 D of the Trade Practices Act.

The Minister for the Industrial Relations, Mr Willis, unveiled the Government's plan to transfer responsibility for secondary boycotts by unions to the Arbitration Commission, at a meeting of the National Labor Consultative Council in Melbourne.

Secondary boycotts are covered by sections 45 D and E of the act giving the Federal Court the power to fine unions that impose bans against a third party not directly involved in an industrial dispute.

The Government agreed to abolish the sections in response to pressure from the ACTU. It plans to amend the Conciliation and Arbitration Act, giving the commission power to call hearings of disputes involving secondary boycotts.

But under the Government's proposed changes the commission could not arbitrate by directing the parties involved in a dispute.

Its powers would be confined to conciliation.

Employer representatives who attended yesterday's meeting told Mr Willis that the Government's proposal was unacceptable because it considerably weakened the sanctions available to companies hit by secondary boycotts.

The employers are seeking the support of the Australian Democrats to block the Government's proposed legislation in the Senate. The Federal Opposition has promised to vote against any changes to the Trade Practices Act.

Fig 24
(Courtesy of The Melbourne Age)

MANAGEMENT

MBA no premium on job market

The possession of an MBA in the US is an automatic ticket to a highly-paid job, but the Australian experience it seems is turning out the reverse.

By HELEN DALLEY

When Hooker Corp chief executive Barry Glover returned to head office after a three-month advanced management course at Harvard in 1981, he was so impressed he determined that Hooker would be "infused" with MBAs — masters of business administration.

At the time Hooker (now ranked 128 in Australia's Top 500 companies), employed no MBAs among its 2600-strong staff in offices around Australia.

Three years later, Hooker still employs no MBAs. Despite Glover's enthusiasm and personal experience the company is "still addressing the problem." Although Hooker intends hiring by year's end, its attitude typifies the present predicament of MBA recruitment.

Like many other companies, Hooker prefers to employ people with various types of tertiary qualifications for a specific job, not just MBAs. Industry supports business degrees, but recruitment of MBAs is more incidental than deliberate.

It is far better in my view to work for oneself in Australia, because one can go as far as possible while keeping one step ahead of the tax man. The only trouble is that most Australians do not have a desire to get out and work hard for themselves. They are trained from an early age to opt for the safety and comfort of secure positions with government, behemoth companies and union protection. It is considered almost a sacrilege to talk of being self-employed. Immigrants to Australia have taught many Australians the benefits of working for themselves as evidenced by the many small businesses operated, nice homes owned by these 'new' Australians, that dot the Australian landscape.

So if one is a lazy worker who likes to sluff off at any given opportunity, staying with the one job for the rest of his life, pack your bags and get on the first Boeing 747 headed for Australia, this will be your paradise! Good luck, because before long you will be complaining along with everybody else about the lousy political, industrial and cost of living problems plaguing the nation, and rounding off the conversation blaming everyone else but yourself for the mess Australia is in.

EMPLOYMENT CONDITIONS AND BENEFITS

CONDITIONS - HOURS

Australia was very aggressive in the establishment of a 40 hour work week. Unfortunately, the unions have pushed so hard in the race for even shorter working hours that many Australians work closer to 35 hours per week. There have even been unbelievable claims by some unions to push for a 32 hour week! Needless to say, there is never any mention of more productivity or wage cuts to compensate for the hour reductions. This type of organized labor thinking is of paramount stupidity and has little regard for even the slightest appreciation of what makes an economy tick.

SALARIES

When one hires on with an employer in Australia, one is told what one will be paid in the vast majority of cases. There is very little room for negotiation of wages at an initial interview. One of the hardest things I had to get used to was the fact that every U.S. employer I have worked for has a question on their application form asking how much one wants to get paid for the job one is applying for. This may be the ultimate indication of a free enterprise society, but Australians expect the government to set the fair wage for what they do and the employer must abide by that 'award'. There is some salary flexibility for experience and education, but there is almost no room for negotiation. In fact, if one individually negotiated outside the 'award' for better pay in a union shop, that would be illegal or dangerous if the word got around.

By comparison, experienced workers in Australia generally receive significantly less pay than their counterparts in the United States. Entry level positions in both professional and non-professional occupations pay a little more in Australia than they do in the U.S. The minimum wage in Australia is approximately $4.00 per hour compared to $3.35 in the U.S.

Comparing other aspects of income differences, in 1982–1983, the average Australian male income was A$342/wk whereas in the same period the average U.S. male income was US365/wk. The average American male though has to pay less taxes and has a higher salary potential than most any Australian employee could ever achieve. (See Figures 25 & 26)

Executive pay

I was interested in reading John Gilmour's attack on the very high salaries paid to senior executives in Australia (18/7/84, page 43) and his remarks that "there is some doubt as to whether most of the well-paid tall poppies deserve or earn their money." Unfortunately, his article from the Bootery is high on emotion and short on facts.

I am reminded of the story about the young boy selling newspapers on the street corner in Sydney. A Rolls-Royce draws up at the traffic lights, whereupon the young paper seller looks at the gleaming vehicle and says "filthy capitalist," and gives the car a kick as it moves off. The same incident happens in New York but this time the young American boy says, "Nice car you have there, Mister. I'm going to have one of these some time."

This story seems to sum up the difference between our philosophies. Instead of admiring individuals who have succeeded and striving to follow suit we seem to want to fire bullets at them.

To return to John Gilmour and his figures of salaries of $100,000 per annum, there are a number of facts that should be made clear.

■ We have the most highly compressed salary structures of any country in the world. Senior executives are relatively poorly paid in Australia. A few years ago McKinsey and Co did some research in various countries on the rates of after-tax earnings of a chief executive of a medium-sized company compared with someone on average industrial earnings (married person with two children). The results were:

Australia	4.5:1
Britain	6:1
W. Germany	12:1
USA	12:1
Italy	14:1
France	22:1

Other figures from other surveys, e.g. the annual international comparison survey of employment conditions abroad, support these findings.

■ Our marginal tax rates are very high and the gross salaries quoted in the Bootery article would look very different if expressed in after-tax figures.

■ Our compressed salary structures are a prime cause of the apparent lack of drive and push for advancement found in Australian executives which is uncharacteristic of the ambitious American or European equivalent.

■ We find difficulty in getting executives to relocate upon a promotion or on a move to another organisation because the so-called increased remuneration in real terms does not compensate.

I know that in a wage-freeze environment these facts may be difficult to swallow, but we have a real need for our senior executives to accept responsibility and equivalent accountability, and to be paid appropriately.

If you look at the responsibility of a chief executive, who may be on a salary of $150,000 a year but who manages an organisation with a total wage bill of around $100 million, then his effect upon the success of the business could be fairly dramatic. If you doubled or trebled the chief executive's salary it would have little effect on the total bill.

GEOFF HINES

Fig 26

WHAT WORKERS MAY GET IN NEXT 18 MONTHS

	P.C. Effect on National Labor Bill	Effect on Labor Bill
WAGE RISES	6-7	$6500m
OTHER BENEFITS Superannuation 5% Health, safety and affirmative action 1% Anomalies and hours reductions 1% Job security 1%	8	$8000 m

Source: Confederation of Australian Industry

Employers resent $8000m for hidden 'wages'

Australia's employers expect to pay national wage rises totalling 6 or 7 per cent in the next 18 months through wage indexation. This will cost them $6500 million and there is little they can do about it.

Fig 27
(Courtesy of The Melbourne Age)

Take for instance an electrician. Considered quite good occupations in both Australia and America, an Australian electrician in the construction trade has little possibility of earning the $15-$20 per hour his American counterpart can while working for someone else. An Australian electrician has to be self-employed to earn this type of money. A supermarket check-out person in Australia has little chance of earning $10 per hour as is easily achieved in the unionised stores in the U.S.

When it comes to second jobs and overtime there is a marked difference in the way Australia deals with this compared to the U.S. In Australia, a second job carries a prohibitive tax of 50%. A worker is considered being greedy wanting two jobs and depriving some unemployed person of one job. The obvious result is not a drop in the number of second jobs or reduction in the unemployment rate, but a big increase in black market second jobs that the employer underpays in cash.

Overtime is taxed at very high rates. Rather than putting you up a single bracket, even a minimal amount of over-time may jump you two brackets in the one pay period.

PENALTY RATES

Penalty rates paid by employers under strict government industrial laws will make most U.S. employers feel quite weak. The Australian labor laws hold hours outside 7am – 5pm to be almost sacred to most workers. These laws also hold Saturdays and Sundays in great reverence, especially in regard to full-time employees. It is considered reasonable only to ask any full-time employee to work Monday thru Friday, eight hours per day somewhere between 7am and 5pm. If an employer should want any full-time, hourly paid employee to work outside these hours then he pays dearly for the privilege. For instance, any overtime worked in any day, that is, in excess of eight hours, must be paid at time-and-a-half, even if the employee doesn't reach forty hours worked in one week. If the full-time employee works on Saturday he must be paid time-and-a-half for the first four hours, then double-time for any hours in excess of four hours that day. This is regardless of the fact that Saturday may be part of the employees forty hour week. On Sundays the employer must pay double time all day, even though the Sunday may be part of an employees forty hour week. The real crunch comes on public holidays, where the employee can easily get double-time-and-a-half for his trouble. Part-time employees fill most all positions in stores that require out of normal hours work, as few penalty rates apply to part-time workers.

PAY INDEXATION

Australia has taken the ultimate step of indexing many wages to the inflation rate. So every six months when the Consumer Price Index is published, a large number of wages are automatically adjusted upward (downward never exists in this system), to help meet the newly inflated cost of living increases. This is a vicious circle that has culminated in a never ending upward wages/costs spiral. In 1986 the government and many employers saw the folly in this system and there is a move afoot to only allow partial increases in relation to the rate of inflation.

BENEFITS - GENERAL

From a U.S. perspective, benefits in the most part are non-existent for most workers in Australia. Non-existent may seem like too harsh a description initially but one can judge for oneself after reading this section. (See Figures 27 & 28)

HOW LABOR COSTS HAVE CHANGED

	SHARE OF TOTAL HOURLY COST OF LABOR		
	1974	1981	1983
WAGES (Inc. overtime, shift allowances.)	77.5	71.3	·65.5
OTHER LABOR COSTS (Payroll taxes, workers' compensation, superannuation etc.)	22.5	28.7	34.5
	100	100	100

Souries: Australian Bureau of Statistics, AIDA survey, Business Council of Australia Survey

Fig 28
(Courtesy of The Melbourne Age)

Longer Easter break not on: employers

The Victorian Employers Federation yesterday opposed a suggestion that Easter Tuesday be made a public holiday and the State Government said only that it would consider the proposal.

The Trades Hall Council secretary, Mr Ken Stone, said yesterday that the union movement probably would approach the Government with the suggestion.

The executive director of the employers federation, Mr Ian Spicer, said yesterday: "At this stage of our economic recovery we need an extra public holiday like we need a hole in the head."

The union proposal would give workers six days off in a row, linking Easter with Anzac Day.

Fig 29
(Courtesy of The Melbourne Age)

VACATIONS

Benefits, in the form of vacations in Australia, will make most U.S. employers shake in their boots. According to Australian industrial law each employee is entitled to four weeks annual vacation, plus while on vacation one is paid 17.5% MORE than when you are at work! Well vacations ARE expensive if no-one told you recently! While I can hear some American employees rubbing their hands with glee, all employers should take a few stiff shots before reading on. Starting from the second year of employment everyone gets his four weeks annual vacation. When one has spent 25 years with the company one still only get four weeks annual vacation, unlike the U.S. where it may start at two weeks and increase one week with each five to ten years service. So far Australia is ahead on vacations especially when one gets paid more for not working while one is on vacation.

Now, when a person stays with a company or government body for ten years he becomes entitled to three months 'long service leave'. That's right folks, another three month vacation in the 11th year of service in addition to the four weeks annual vacation, plus the 17.5% extra on top of one's normal pay! So in the 11th year of service an employer has to pay his employees 12 months pay for only working 32 weeks. Sounds pretty good to employees so far? Then, after each five more years service with the same company, one receives another 6 weeks long service leave. A real bonanza for the employees it seems. All in all when you make a direct comparison between the average Australian employee and his American counterpart, the Australian gets 54% MORE vacation and 71% MORE vacation pay if both were to stay with a company for 21 years. WOW! That sounds absolutely outstanding! What is the catch? Wait just a moment, there is more.

PUBLIC HOLIDAYS

Public Holidays must also be considered as another form of vacation available to workers in both Australia and the U.S. In the U.S. there are approximately eight public holidays that most employees receive. In Australia most employees receive at least 11 public holidays each year. (See Figure 29) These extra three public holidays per year cost Australia approximately A$1,000,000,000 per year in productivity. If the U.S. were to adopt three extra public holidays per year the nation would lose US$15,000,000,000 per year in productivity.

SICK PAY

Sick Pay benefits is another area that may seem very attractive from the Australian point of view. Most Australians are entitled to two weeks full-pay plus two weeks half-pay per year sick pay. The usual requirement that covers such benefits is that employers insist that one produce a medical certificate from a doctor only if one has more than three consecutive days off sick.

Unfortunately for the Australian nation, 'The Sickie', as it is known, is one of the national past times. Most sick pay benefits are cumulative year to year, but this does not stop the average Australian from using up his yearly allowance regardless of whether he is really sick or not.

So on top of vastly more vacation and more public holidays than the average American sees, Australian employers have to pay another two to three weeks pay per year for their not-so-sick employees abusing their over-generous sick pay benefits. This costs the country a fortune in productivity which translates directly into high prices for goods and services.

While the vacation, public holiday and sick pay analysis looks great for employees, it is disastrous for employers and ultimately works against all Australians in hidden ways. Employers have to build much higher margins into their products and services to support employee benefit costs that now reach 40%+ of the basic salary paid each employee, compared to the U.S. level of almost 20% of salary. Consequently, goods and services cost more than they would otherwise, and wages are kept relatively regulated, allowing little chance for most people to make great gains from year to year based on job performance and productivity, as can be achieved by many of their U.S. counterparts. Australia may be ahead when it comes to vacations but is the price they pay worth it? I think not. Between the cost of living and the tax man, Australia as a nation gains virtually nothing by this vacation glut.

RETIREMENT

Retirement benefits come in various, not universal forms in Australia. Many companies and all government bodies offer 'superannuation' plans. These are simply contributory retirement plans for the benefit of the employees to supplement their social security retirement incomes. The employee puts a weekly amount in the account and the employer usually matches that amount with an equivalent or slightly better contribution. The employee is taxed on the contribution when it goes in AND also when it is withdrawn for retirement income. There is some averaging that goes on but this is a rather draconian tax measure in most people's estimation. For a great number of employees there is no plan offered by their employers and they must make their own arrangements if they are to have a comfortable retirement income in addition to their social security income. I had never heard of a non-contributory

57

retirement program until I came to the U.S. It is not surprising that these non–contributory programs are not set up in Australia, considering the amount of money the employer has to pay in vacation benefits.

MEDICAL/DENTAL COVERAGE

As for free or subsidized employee medical, dental and optical insurance coverage programs, the only people who routinely receive these benefits are middle management employees of rather large companies. Australia claims to have a socialised medical program but it is a must for the average person to purchase medical coverage for themselves and their family if they want to avoid being crippled by excessive medical costs and have access to the best medical care.

Australians make a killing in vacations, but it costs a great deal as evidenced by the lack of other standard benefits most Americans take for granted.

Chapter
Five

Business
In
Australia

WHO OWNS AUSTRALIAN BUSINESS?

Much of Australia's big business consists of foreign owned multinational corporations. The home of most multinationals is Britain, U.S. and Japan. Australia is also a land of small business like the U.S. with every type of business falling into this category.

There are numerous Australian-owned big businesses, mainly in the hands of Australia's old time wealthy families who got their start years ago and whose roots are firmly planted in Britain.

The majority of big business the average Australian is exposed to, is in the retail areas, so it is to be expected that many U.S. companies are household names to Australians. Safeway, McDonalds, Kentucky Fried, K Mart, Target, Waltons, Esso, Mobil, Caltex (Texaco), Amoco, GE, General Motors, Ford, Colgate-Palmolive, Alka Seltzer, Kraft, Columbia Records, 3M, IBM, HP, Motorola and many more American identities are readily recognized. The reason foreign owned companies are so popular is that Australia has encouraged foreign business (not financial) investors to come to Australia for many years. In the last few years Australia has just begun to encourage the influx of foreign capital by allowing the limited establishment of foreign banking interests in Australia. Undoubtedly a move in the best long-term interests of Australia, albeit 100 years too late.

Venture capital is a relatively new concept in Australian business life. The usual deal the Australian government would cut with foreign companies is that if they set up manufacturing operations in Australia the vast majority of their earnings would not attract Australian business taxes in exchange for the creation of jobs. The alternative to manufacturing goods in Australia for a foreign based company is to import what the company wishes to sell. If the foreign business just sets up distribution networks for imported goods, then the government heavily taxes all the products imported, in the hope that these products will then be less competitive than Australian manufactured goods. Nice in theory but it does not work in practice.

It is no wonder the majority of foreign owned multinationals in Australia manufacture all or part of their product line inside Australia. One of the problems with this theory is the fact that foreign owned multinational companies may have provided some jobs, but they have exported vast amounts of income with the Australian people seeing very little benefit in government tax revenues or extensive reinvestment in Australia. The Australian public criticize the companies for this situation rather than their own politicians who created and perpetuate the system of foreign investment in Australia.

Australia created this situation of ever decreasing ownership of its resources because they failed to allow large scale foreign capital investment and also failed to create a taxation system that would have allowed Australian entrepreneurs to exploit foreign financial resources to build Australian majority owned businesses.

Australians love to hate big businesses; the bigger and more foreign-owned, the more they love to hate them. The Australian public is much less sophisticated than the American public when it comes to dealing with business investments. Where the average American looks on IBM, AT&T and the like with a 'I wish I had a goodly amount of stock in that company', many millions of Australians castigate their own big companies with a 'Bloody dirty great capitalists ripping us poor bastards off the first chance they get, and I don't want to be involved in that!' attitude.

PROTECTIONISM IN AUSTRALIA

The hairs on my neck stand on end every time I hear Americans calling for protection of various American industries. Australia is a fine example of where active protectionism will lead an industrialized western nation. First, most everything costs more than it should if a country practices substantial protectionism. There really isn't any such thing as non–substantial protectionism because when a country starts it usually gets hooked, and before long everyone wants to be protected from imports. If most everything costs more then the entire population is losing for a lifetime.

Let me relate the story as I understand it of roughly what happened when Ford, General Motors and Chrysler demanded, and received, government protection from foreign imports for their Australian operations.

Australia imported most all its cars in the very early years from Britain and the U.S. because there was no viable large scale automobile production in Australia. During the first half of this century, the Australian automotive manufacturing industry, which consisted mainly of small manufacturers, was bought out by or consolidated under the American big three and a few big British names. Following this industry shake out came the demand for protection of Australian jobs from cheap foreign auto imports. Foreign based manufacturers were able to produce cars cheaper by sheer economy of scale in comparison to Australia's relatively small overall demand for vehicles. Sounds good in theory.

The government got involved when the 'Big Three' doubtless with the help of the trade unions, more or less threatened to withdraw from manufacturing in

Australia if they didn't get protection. The government agreed to impose import duties and tariffs on nearly all foreign auto imports. This sounded good in practice but the result was a general disaster for the Australian consumer of motor vehicles, and a financial bonanza for the Australian based manufacturers and the federal treasury.

Today the Australian auto industry is protected in this manner; all imported cars FOB (fresh off the boat) attract import duties of 90% of their value! If the car is brought in in parts, called a CKU (completely knocked down unit), it attracts a 45% import duty. Also, new car sales for any given year cannot exceed 20% foreign cars. There is no way this limit can be varied without government directives.

This is what results from all this protectionism: An imported car for instance may cost the Australian importer $4000 from the manufacturer in Japan. When that car arrives in Australia, the importer has to then pay the Australian Government $3600 import duty. The car's cost to the importer is $7600. The importer may add say 10% importer's margin which brings it to $8360. Then the dealer may add another say 15% for the dealer's margin on each car bringing this to $9614. Everyone then has to pay 15% sales tax on car sales inflating this once $4000 vehicle to a retail price of $11,000+.

My figures may not be perfectly accurate in this instance, but one can get the idea of what happens with a protection system as developed in Australia. Crucial to fully understanding the implications of this system of protection, is that Australian based companies are now manufacturing similar cars with cheaper labor than most of their import competition. The similar Australian built cars come off the production line costing about the same $4000 that the imports initially cost. Do you think Australian manufacturers are going to add a few hundred dollars margin to their cars and sell them thousands of dollars cheaper than the competition just to move volume? No way! The Australian manufacturers grossly inflate the wholesale and retail cost of their vehicles and make huge profit margins, ripping off the general population, not worrying about becoming overly competitive, all in the noble cause of protecting Australian jobs. A national fraud of the grossest proportions that very little is being done to correct. There are too many people profiting, government included! Ford and GM regularly cite their Australian operations among their most profitable overseas operations.

Protectionism also applies to most all other products. The theory goes that the government has to place significant import duties on all manner of goods to protect Australian jobs from cheap foreign labor. The net result, as mentioned earlier, is not so much protecting jobs but allowing businesses to be less competitive than they otherwise would have to be, and all Australians are paying more for goods than they would in a more free enterprise economy. The list of protected goods is virtually endless with import duties ranging from 15%-150% of the original value of the goods.

FARMERS AND EXPORTERS

These Australian business people could be said to have it made in the shade. Australia has always gone out of its way to excessively support farmers and exporters, to the general detriment of the greater population, much the same way as the U.S. government has at times.

If a farmer grows wheat or wool he can only sell his crop to a government body that guarantees a certain price before the crop is produced.(Talking about wool as a crop is convenient at this point). Wheat growers are given quotas for their farm and all production up to that quota is guaranteed to be purchased and paid for at a fixed amount REGARDLESS of domestic economic conditions or international wheat prices. Any excess production above the quota is usually purchased by the Wheat Board at a slightly lower rate then quota wheat. I believe it is illegal for a farmer to sell wheat on the open market. Similarly, sheep ranchers are given quotas for wool production and guaranteed prices when another government body, The Wool Board, buys their annual production.

After these government bodies have purchased the wheat and wool crops they resell them to the domestic and world markets and pocket any profits that may be involved, or take any losses that may occur. Needless to say, this is a gravy situation for wheat and wool growers in Australia, they can't lose. (See Figure 30)

Dairy farmers are another highly protected group. While dairy farmers sell their products to dairies seemingly in a more or less open market situation, they are subsidized very heavily indirectly, with guarantees to dairies by the government regarding production levels and purchasing of excess milk products in the form of powdered milk and cheese, very similar to the U.S. system of dairy farm subsidies. The rationalization for this protection and squandering of taxpayers' monies on a selected few business people is that it keeps prices stable and makes sure these farmers stay in business, regardless of the economic climates that would otherwise effect their production and efficiency. This situation allows too many small and very inefficient farms to stay in business at great consumer expense. No wonder a gallon of milk costs $2.98! (See Figure 31)

WHEAT PAYMENTS

THE Australian Wheat Board has made a further payment of $5 a tonne for all wheat delivered to the 1982-83 Wheat Pool.

The board's acting general manager, Mr M. Connell, said a further payment of around $2.50 a tonne could be expected in September.

Since the Guaranteed Minimum Price was paid, subsequent pool payments (including the present $5 a tonne) for 1982-83 wheat now total $16.50 a tonne.

Fig 30
(Courtesy of The Melbourne Age)

Federal aid sought to fight subsidised EEC products

CANBERRA. — The National Party has called on the Hawke Government to help fund an independent attempt by primary industry groups to undercut popular support for subsidised European Economic Community farm exports.

Fig 31
(Courtesy of The Melbourne Age)

Exporters operate under amazingly preferential conditions compared to regular domestic business. Many multinational companies have mining operations in coal, iron ore, nickel and bauxite. As most of this material is exported in its raw state, the exporters get very attractive tax breaks and even more preferential treatment if they are foreign-owned. Other smaller Australian industries that export receive preferential tax treatment from the government as an incentive to export, thus producing more Australian jobs than the economy could otherwise support. So the Australian government runs this great scam where it taxes most all imports very heavily, then gives great benefits to companies that export from Australia. The government wants it both ways, but the consumer and average tax payer end up paying for it all in higher prices for non-competitive Australian made goods and tax subsidies for the exporters. (See Figure 32)

GOVERNMENT BUSINESSES

What businesses do the Australian federal and state governments run? Just about every type of large service business you can think of. Here is a list and brief description of the businesses federal and state governments are involved in:

BANKING

The Commonwealth Bank, owned and operated by a federal government body, is the largest bank in Australia. Each state government has its own bank operating within state boundaries and usually in the capital cities of other states . (The rest of the banking business is privately owned and very heavily regulated. Foreign banking was introduced on a limited basis during 1984.)

AIRLINES

QANTAS Airlines, Australia's ONLY international air carrier is a federal government business. Australia Airlines (AA) is a domestic carrier owned and operated by the federal government.

COMMODITIES

As mentioned previously, The Australian Wheat Board and The Australian Wool Board purchase just about all wheat and wool produced in Australia, then sell it off to domestic and international markets at auction.

RAIL TRANSPORTATION

The Australian National Railways is a federal government business operating trans continental passenger services (like AMTRAK), national freight services (like CONRAIL), and also operates the state passenger and freight rail services of the Northern Territory, South Australia and Tasmania. Each of the remaining states operates its own passenger and freight services on a statewide basis, not regional transit basis as is the case in the U.S. There are no privately owned rail systems in Australia except those in the large strip mining areas for bulk ore transportation.

MEDICAL INSURANCE

Medibank, a federal national health scheme, was set up in 1973 by the feds and worked very effectively and efficiently for a number of years before successive administrations got to it and destroyed it for philosophical reasons. In past few years, Medicare has risen from the ashes only to be regarded as a very inadequate and half-baked excuse for a national health scheme. The federal government also operates

The export gravy train

● The Federal Government's export incentives scheme has been a lucrative source of funds for some of Australia's richest companies.

Fig 32
(Courtesy of The Melbourne Age)

Treasurer calls Kennett's SIO scheme asinine

A proposal by the Opposition Leader, Mr Kennett, to sell the State Insurance Office to private enterprise was an "asinine comment" designed to make political capital, the Treasurer, Mr Jolly, said yesterday.

Mr Jolly said Mr Kennett's proposal reflected his "abysmal ignorance of economic issues" and could cost each taxpayer at least another $100 a year.

Fig 33
(Courtesy of The Melbourne Age)

a private health insurance company in direct competition with private health care insurers.

LIABILITY INSURANCE

The State Insurance Office is a common state run business. When one registers a motorvehicle in Australia, one automatically pays liability insurance at the same time and place to the Department of Motor Vehicles. This no-fault insurance is provided by each state as a business proposition. Private insurance companies were once in this field but one no longer has a choice in the matter. (See Figure 33)

ELECTRICITY AND HEATING GAS

Each state owns and operates its electric and gas utilities and provides services to the communities. Again, these operations do not necessarily run profitably or efficiently, and the tax payer/rate payer has to make up the loss. There are no large, privately owned electricity and gas utilities in Australia. Electricity and gas are no cheaper because of state ownership. The reverse is true as these utilities do not have to answer to any Public Utilities Commission before raising service and supply rates. (See Figure 34)

WATER AND SEWAGE

These services are provided by the state run or city/county run utilities and once again are not required to run efficiently or profitably, the tax payer picking up any short falls and paying for the inefficiency of government operations.

TELEPHONE

Telecom Australia, as the federal government telephone company is known, runs all telecommunications inside Australia, and the government controls most all overseas telecommunications also. This is a very profitable business always ending each financial year with huge surpluses at user and tax payer expense. Even compared to the deregulated U.S. telecommunications industry, Telecom is expensive and inefficient when it comes to customer service and charges. (See Figure 35)

TELEVISION AND RADIO

The federal government owns and operates two of the five national television networks; the remaining three are privately owned and heavily regulated. The federal government also operates two national radio networks. All the government networks are run at great expense to the tax payers who provide 100% of the operating revenues.

LIGHT RAIL AND BUS SERVICES

Many states operate all the local commuter light rail and bus services without direct competition from private sources. If the state doesn't run the service, then it is common for private operators to run commuter services subsidized by the government. It has been shown in numerous Australian studies that private bus companies can provide local and long distance bus services at approximately half the cost per passenger mile than those provided by the government.

POSTAL SERVICES

Australia Post is the federal government's attempt to provide an efficient postal service. In this day and age, many mailmen still ride bicycles or walk their routes in suburban areas, making them inconceivably inefficient compared to their U.S. counterparts. It

HEC attacked on prices

The Tasmanian Hydro-Electric Commission was selling power at half cost in an effort to rid itself of an embarrassing surplus of hydro-electricity, the Wilderness Society claimed yesterday.

Fig 34
(Courtesy of The Melbourne Age)

Dial a cheapie for a buzz

Telecom is moving to have banned some imported telephones which it claims are poor-quality, unsafe and in some cases might send a 240-volt shock down the line.

Telecom's public relations director, Mr Brian Luscombe, said yesterday that he would have talks with the Department of Industry and Commerce to consider banning some imports.

"They could be electrically unsafe, could cause wrong numbers to be dialled and have a high rate of mechanical breakdown," he said.

Telecom also announced yesterday that Australia would be one of the first countries to have push-button electronic telephones as basic units in homes from September.

The new phones will be installed with new connections and are expected to replace rotary-dial telephones over the next 10 years. They look like standard touch telephones, but have a re-dial facility which re-calls the last number dialled.

Telecom plans to change public and red rotary telephones over to push-button, and will investigate credit-card public telephones.

Meanwhile, Mr Luscombe has warned subscribers against buying sub-standard imported phones, some of which sell for as little as $20. Telecom flip-phones, which have a warranty, sell for $69.

Mr Luscombe denied that the crackdown was a move to protect Telecom's monopoly. He displayed several telephones which had been the subject of complaints to Telecom. One example, he said, could send a 240-volt shock down the line.

Sixty companies hold Telecom permits for 253 different telephones. From July, all the permits will require annual renewal.

Fig 35
(Courtesy of The Melbourne Age)

may be quaint for them to walk and use bicycles but one pays 30 cents for domestic letters and twice as much as the U.S. rates for international mail. There is of course no obligation for Australia Post to operate at the break even point as the U.S. Postal Service is required to do.

ROAD CONSTRUCTION AND MAINTENANCE

The Department of Main Roads or The Country Roads Board are familiar state run operations that not only maintain roads as does CALTRANS here in California, but these state bodies also build many roads. Little construction work on major roads is performed by private construction companies. As there is little or no private bidding on road construction projects, the government workers and their managers on each construction site are under no obligation to work efficiently or economically.

One now should have an appreciation of why the Australian government workforces are so large and understand why services cost more despite the public/state ownership of vast amounts of business activities. Never let anyone convince you that governments are capable of running any kind of business more efficiently than someone with a profit motive; such thinking is pure bunk!

TRANSPORTATION

This overall subject requires somewhat more elaboration because it is the root of many of Australia's inherent problems.

As the government is in control of most all forms of public transportation, there are some self fulfilling prophecies that go along with the situation. The road systems in Australia's cities and countryside are positively atrocious in terms of construction and maintenance compared to those in the U.S. The Australian public owns motorvehicles at about the same rate per 100,000 population as do people in the U.S., and they also like to drive them just about as much as their U.S. cousins.

Unfortunately, from the government's point of view, if people drive their cars in the cities to commute to work, this loss of patronage hurts the state owned public transport. As it is currently, nearly 80% of all commuting passenger miles are made by car in Australian cities. Australians pay exceedingly high prices for gasoline because of the enormous government taxes levied on the fuel; but the government, rather than directing this tax revenue toward road construction and maintenance, utilizes it primarily for subsidizing public transport or adds it to the general revenues. So even though the transportation of choice is the automobile, all drivers heavily support inefficient public transport systems that most never use. More to the point is the fact that these huge public transport systems are generally grossly inefficient and become bottomless pits for tax payers' dollars. There are very few attempts to really streamline and modernize the management and facilities of these systems so that they become much less of a drain on the public purse. (See Figure 36)

Interstate bus services are run by private enterprise operations such as Greyhound and Ansett Pioneer. There is relatively little regulation of these services because the government is not competing directly.

The internal airlines are dominated by Ansett, a private company, and Australia Airlines (AA), a federal government business operation. Prices and schedules are more or less fixed by government order allowing little or no competition, the schedules for each airline are only minutes apart for the same destinations. This ensures no real competition

Maclellan gets that sinkhole feeling

The deputy State Opposition leader and former Transport Minister, Mr Rob Maclellan, yesterday made the embarrassing admission that under his administration, Vic Rail lost $449.50 a minute, making it "Australia's deepest cash sinkhole".

Fig 36
(Courtesy of The Melbourne Age)

Fares fair in air: 'Choice'

The rising cost of domestic air fares has made many Australians decide to leave flying to the birds. But according to 'Choice' magazine, we pay less to fly than most other people in the world — including Americans.

HOW WE RATE

FLIGHTS	DISTANCE (KM)	ECONOMY FARE $A	CENTS/ KM
Melbourne-Sydney	707	133.30	18.85
London-Lyon	732	185.12	25.28
Sydney-Adelaide	1166	182.50	15.65
Chicago-Hartford	1261	229.37	18.18
Adelaide-Perth	2120	266.50	12.57
Los Angeles-New Orleans	2692	388.08	14.41
Hobart-Darwin	3882	382.50	9.85
London-Tel Aviv	3575	733.94	20.52

The article said that Australians tended to think local fares were expensive because they compared them to the cheapest available discount fares overseas, many of which had stringent conditions attached.

"When Australians are planning an overseas trip they often shop around for the best available fare, but when flying at home they often don't ask about discounts," the article said.

The article said Australian taxpayers subsidised air fares, but the majority of those taxpayers never flew. Only about 15 per cent of Australians used the airlines, and only about 3 per cent flew regularly.

Fig 37
(Courtesy of The Melbourne Age)

throughout Australia and the traveler is stuck with what is offered. I believe that the government's only reason for fixing fares and schedules is that AA would be miserably inefficient compared to Ansett in a free market situation and AA would go bankrupt. There has been some recent competition on some of the main trunk routes, such as Melbourne – Sydney, but these smaller airlines must stop somewhere between the two cities to allow them to operate on the trunk routes.

A worse situation exists when it comes to international airlines in Australia. There is only one Australian owned and operated international airline, QANTAS. The trouble is it is owned and operated by the Australian federal government. Similar to the domestic airline regulation, the government more or less fixes fares and schedules for international airlines servicing Australia. By government decree, an international airline could not even be started in Australia that competed with QANTAS. QANTAS is a money losing behemoth as it stands, absorbing vast amounts of tax revenues just to stay afloat.

The federal government cannot run its' operations at a profit so they fix airfares and schedules to squash competition. This results in Australians paying exorbitantly high airfares inside and outside Australia. A recent (1984) comparison of airfares around the world by CHOICE Magazine, Australia's equivalent to Consumer Reports Magazine, was published in the Melbourne Age and claimed Australia had very competitive airfares. As one can see from this report, airfares were compared on similar mileage journeys only, not on whether the route was a high density trunk route with the same air mileage. For example, there should have been an example of Melbourne – Sydney compared to Los Angeles – San Francisco, and also Sydney – Perth compared to New York – San Francisco for a true picture of cost comparisons. This is just another subtle way by which the Australian people are snowed by their media into thinking they have got it really good compared to the rest of the world, when in fact the truth is being conveniently distorted to suit the government's purposes. (See Figure 37)

The best thing that could happen to air transport in Australia would be to put AA and QANTAS on the stock market to 'privatize' them, then have strong anti-trust laws to monitor the industry to make sure it really is competing for business. (See Figure 38)

BANKING

Banking in Australia, dominated by the federal government, deserves a closer look to provide a clearer picture of how this government manipulation has served to wreck Australia's development over the years.

As the Commonwealth Bank, owned and operated by the federal government, controls more banking transactions in Australia than all other banks combined, there has been for many years an incredibly tight regulation of the banking industry. Interest rates are fixed by the federal government from what can be paid on deposits to what can be charged on loans.

This heavy regulation virtually shut out all foreign banking interests that wanted to invest cold hard cash in the Australian economy. The federal government instead settled for attracting multinational, capital-rich companies rather than let foreign bankers finance Australian owned business ventures. This had a detrimental effect on Australia's development that I feel is almost impossible to reverse. Venture capital was not even a part of the Australian language, when American businesses were moving mountains in the high tech revolution financed primarily by venture capital. Australia just recently (1984) opened up business investment and venture capital markets to foreign bankers; but most average banking services are still off limits to foreign owned banks, probably because they could compete very effectively with the federal and state government–owned banks.

A Building Society is the Australian equivalent of a Savings and Loan and represents really the only non–bank banking in Australia. The other dozen or so private banks in Australia have recently undergone mergers into larger Australian–owned units probably as a shield against the new foreign competitors that have set up shop in Australia. It is a great pity that American banks are not allowed to offer regular banking services to the Australian public because the Australia banks would then find out what good customer service is really like!

The government regulation of interest rates sounds great, except that they never seem to go down. Interest rates are immune to the wild fluctuations that can be experienced in the U.S., but they always creep upwards in a non–competitive, never ending spiral. To my knowledge, there is no such thing as a thirty year fixed interest rate mortgage in Australia. As the federal government is heavily involved in the banking business, it will never see fit to make mortgage interest, or any interest for that matter, tax deductible for the average non–business person as it is here in the U.S.

IS AUSTRALIAN BUSINESS REALLY FREE ENTERPRISE?

When I lived in Australia I thought that the country was a free enterprise society and even sometimes TOO free enterprise when it came to the multinational corporate interests.

No more! When looked at closely, using the U.S. as a free enterprise model (although some may disagree with this analysis of the U.S.) Australia is far from a free enterprise economy. On the contrary, I believe Australia should be described as a borderline western socialist economy that appears to be free enterprise oriented but actively discouraging free enterprise in the infrastructure of its own society. The bottom line to this whole business picture is that the consumer is paying dearly for excessively priced goods and is being taxed heavily to support those state-run businesses and government largesse. This is a far from satisfactory situation for any country but especially for Australia with its enormous productive potential.

Beazley to look at US air fare cuts

The Minister for Aviation, Mr Beazley, has expressed concern about Qantas's ability to cope with increasingly cut-throat competition on the US route.

He says that in the next few weeks he will look closely at the treaties which cover the rights of all airlines on the route, and consider carefully the Government's role in protecting Qantas.

Fig 38
(Courtesy of The Melbourne Age)

Chapter
Six

Consumerism

PRODUCTS AND THEIR ORIGINS

One may have gotten the impression in the early chapters that Australian stores must be full of Australian–made products with very few imports adorning the shelves. This is not the case, much to the disappointment of a government that would prefer to see as many Australian made goods as possible in the stores.

Even though imports carry high duties and high sales taxes when sold in Australia, imports are as prevalent, if not more prevalent than are imports in the U.S. It seems that as protection, taxes and inflation go higher and higher, more and more Australian jobs are lost to foreign manufacturers and imports grow to fill this void for lack of Australian manufactures. I do not know why this happens, but there seems to be some sort of inverse law at work here. The theory Australia has worked with for years was supposed to protect Australian jobs and increase the availability of Australian–made products to the Australian public. It is quite difficult to find a wide range of domestically made goods at reasonable prices unlike here in the U.S. Reasonable prices are the key here. Taxes, unions and unwarranted regulation play such a big role in the Australian economy that what would otherwise be quality products produced at reasonable costs, become overpriced in the market place and fall victim to equal quality imports at lower prices.

WHERE DO THE DOLLARS GO?

Sales tax on any item purchased can range from 7% minimum to 32.5% maximum, depending on the category of goods you purchase.

For instance, jewelry, silverware, pens, watches, cosmetics, shampoo and conditioners, shaving cream and razors, photographic equipment and film, record and tape players, tapes and records, radios, TV's and VCR's all attract the horrendous sales tax of 32.5%!

Household furniture, drapes, carpets, airconditioners, dishwashers, hand tools, and garage tools attract a more reasonable sales tax of only 7.5%. However, when purchasing cars, the sales tax, which is not tax deductible, runs a staggering 15%! An American can usually buy up to 50%+ more product for his money than the average Australian.

STORE HOURS

At the time of writing, most stores in Australia are forced by trading laws to keep maximum hours of 9am–6pm M–F and 8am–1pm Saturday. Except for 7/11 type stores, restaurants and the three nights a week for supermarkets, all other businesses not in designated tourist areas cannot conduct retail or industrial sales business outside of regular business hours because it is against the law! (See Figure 39)

There are a number of very bad reasons for this state of affairs that need explaining. First, there is the British tradition of restricting trading hours because this is a civilized thing to do, especially on Sundays, which should be totally off limits to all trading in respect of The Lords Day. Ironically, Britain has a tradition of all day Saturday trading and half a day one other week day. Why this didn't carry over to Australia I'll never know.

Second, it has to do with the trade unions. The trade unions consider anything out of regular hours M–F as sacred time for their members. The Retail Clerks Union for many years has always wanted its members paid penalty rates for working other than regular hours, regardless of whether or not those

Trading

The State Opposition Leader, Mr Kennett, said in a radio broadcast last night that a Liberal Government would "totally deregulate shop trading. Shops may be open 24 hours a day, seven-days-a-week, as and when they choose to. It will provide jobs, at least 25,000 jobs, almost immediately in retailing and supporting industry and services".

Fig 39
(Courtesy of The Melbourne Age)

Citizen Cain

from M. Urwin

While plucky Penhalluriack fights to keep his store open and resists the ridiculous Victorian trading hours, Citizen Cain proposes allowing the pubs to stay open on Sundays.

Extended shopping hours are a harmless convenience for those unable to shop during regular hours. Extended drinking hours can only exacerbate an already chronic problem in the community of alcohol abuse, addiction and road accidents.

MAVIS URWIN,
Mont Albert.

Fig 40
(Courtesy of The Melbourne Age)

hours make up the union members forty hours per week. (See Figure 40)

Many businesses got over this problem by hiring more part-time workers to handle the couple of late nights and Saturday mornings that they could operate. Trade unions hate part-time workers because they rarely, if ever, join unions. But, it still prevails that many retail clerks jobs are held by union members that absolutely refuse to work other hours as their regular forty, and their union and the governments back them up in this regard.

Third, the reason this still goes on regardless of public sentiment to the contrary, is that there is no way for the public to change the system. Petitions and propositions are not a working part of any Australian government process, therefore the people are in the hands of the politicians, prisoners of their own votes so to speak. (See Figure 41)

In the most unbelievable case against free enterprise ever seen in Australia, Mr. Penhalluriack, a Melbourne hardware store owner, was jailed and fined $500,000 for operating his store on Saturdays and Sundays in a non-designated tourist area. Never mind the fact that when I visited this store in 1980 on a Saturday afternoon it was packed with customers who couldn't wait to buy everything that they could get their hands on.

The Labor government in Victoria, being in the hands and pockets of the trade unions, persecuted this family owned business for nothing more than spite. The store owner was providing the public with a much needed service - what's more basic than hardware items available on week-ends?, and they jailed him! As this enormous fine was handed down when we were there in August 1984, I wondered very seriously about whether we had come back to a communist ruled country! (See Figure 42)

By the end of 1986 this feisty martyr for the cause of free enterprise was still collecting fines and still selling hardware on weekends after the jail term didn't stick. More power to Mr. Penhalluriack.

The main problem that arises with these ridiculous store hours is if both family members work regular hours, as most Australians do. One then has to rush around on Saturday morning or till 9pm on a couple of nights during the week to get the shopping done. The fact that everyone else is out there trying to do the same thing means that it is one big mess all year round. It makes one's pace of life very fast. (See Figure 43)

While we were visiting in 1984, there was an attempt in New South Wales to get extended trading hours, as they are called, but the government had to go cap-in-hand to the unions to ask permission to let businesses open later and on week-ends. Who would hear such a thing? The government and unions giving permission to business to practice free enterprise? Amazing!

When we left in 1981, Tasmania, which was the only state with unlimited trading hours, actually reversed their laws. Under direct pressure from the trade unions, the government made it illegal to trade out of regular hours as established on the mainland! I used to think Tasmanians were a little backward in their thinking, but that really takes the cake. In conclusion, store hours in Australia are a big pain and make life much more complicated than it need be.

Beer but not hardware on a Sunday

from R. N. Wolstenholme

I read with disgust in the morning papers today (6/10) the news that the State Government will soon be giving hotels the go for Sunday trading. I am not disgusted at the fact that the people of Victoria will be permitted to grace the bar of their local watering hole without having to purchase food, but more so that the State Government has indicated that there will be higher penalties for the many hardware retailers and other shopkeepers who give service to the community, by opening their doors on a Sunday, and in return are fined by the Department of Labor and Industry.

Fig 41
(Courtesy of The Melbourne Age)

Trading fines
prove expensive

The State Government collected more than $220,000 in fines for breaches of the weekend trading laws last year.

Fig 42
(Courtesy of The Melbourne Age)

MONEY

Australia is still very much a cash oriented society, coming into the credit world rather slowly compared to the U.S.

Gas credit cards were the preserve of the business few until a few years ago. Australia, for all intents and purposes, actually by–passed the gas credit card and has moved straight into debit cards at the gas pump as a means of convenience. I personally think this is a rip–off because the gas in no cheaper using a debit card than if you pay by cash or regular bank credit card.

Store credit cards are not all that prevalent because there are not as many large chain stores in Australia as in America. But the most amazing lack of sophistication Australia shows is its paranoia about personal checks.

Checks are an accepted form of payment for bills of a regular nature, like phone, utilities etc., but are looked upon with a jaundiced eye when it comes to transactions for general merchandise. One wouldn't think of buying groceries and getting cash back with a check, unless it was government issued and one possessed a veritable dossier of personal identification. Many store people are very uncomfortable around checks and most stores will not accept personal checks regardless of the amount of solid I.D. you carry. Travelers checks are the exception to this rule because they are considered as good as cash.

Many employees, even of larger businesses, are still paid their salary in cash every pay day! This is a real anachronism, but it is a sign of how unsophisticated Australians are about money.

Another aspect about spending money in Australia. The Australian currency is the Australian dollar. The government once levied a tax of 12 cents for every check written, perhaps this is why checks never gained universal popularity in Australia. This was recently done away with to be replaced by transaction taxes on every financial transaction involving a bank account. So now when an Australian deposits money in his own bank account (even his own pay check) and when he withdraws money or just transfers funds between accounts, the federal and state government get a minute amount of taxation, pennies. Multiply these pennies on every transaction in Australia and it soon becomes an enormous revenue source for the taxation department. This form of taxation is known as the 'Stuff the Mattress' and 'Under the Floor Boards' tax system, indicating what many Australians now do with their savings to avoid paying these draconian taxes.

SERVICE AUSTRALIAN STYLE

The visitor to Australia should be well prepared for a shock when it comes to customer service.

In supermarkets for instance, the customers cart is NEVER unloaded by the clerk, and more often than not one has to BAG HIS OWN groceries! The most significant difference at the check-out, apart from what was just mentioned, is that very few clerks greet the customer or smile and indulge in small talk to make this mundane shopping exercise any more pleasant. When we were there in July–August 1984, only one Safeway check-out clerk made our shopping a pleasant experience. We very much missed the normal 'Have a Nice Day', especially when we felt most all clerks were thinking 'Give me your money and get out of my face!'. When one is inside the supermarkets, there is rarely an 'excuse me' or 'thank you' from other shoppers after they bash into you with their carts or after you politely make room in an aisle so they can pass.

If one thinks that tipping is a rip–off, let me tell you about eating out in Australia where tipping is not the norm.   Tipping is not everyday practice in Australia. Waiters and waitresses are paid more than the minimum wage, probably double the minimum wage is more like it. Rather than receiving superior service as logic may suggest due to the far higher basic wage, the effect on service is dramatic in the absence of tipping.   As waiters or waitresses have nothing to gain in most cases by giving top class service, 'You get what you pay for'.   Service in Australian restaurants is generally slow and below average compared to even the most modest eating establishments in the U.S.   The real forces at work in these situations is that the person serving gets paid the same amount for serving one customer or one hundred during that shift.   When I first visited the U.S. I was adamant that I was not going to tip anyone because I thought that the pay should be enough for the job done.   It was not long before I realized just how great American service is in most areas and I began to tip for the appropriate services and from then on expected top class service all the time and became disgruntled if I didn't get it.   On our recent trip back to Australia we really missed even the moderately good service we are so used to in the U.S.

Australians paranoia of tipping was exhibited to us when we left a small tip to a particularly good waitress in a well known cafe in downtown Melbourne. The person that took our place as we left looked in disgust at the tip and we would have been dead if looks could kill.   The customers look said it all, 'Bloody tourists, they will spoil it for the rest of us.'

Service in almost all aspects of Australian business is less than satisfactory when compared to even the most modest U.S. standards. It seems as though most business people outside of the tourist industry have the attitude that, 'Business would be great if it wasn't for the bloody customers!' In fact, many Australians who work for themselves take the attitude that they should be able to live and work like they were working for someone else.

One might think that any business offering great service would make a killing in Australia. In fact, that is not too far from the truth. Many Australians object to American businesses such as Safeway, McDonalds, K Mart and the like, because they feel they have depersonalized shopping and give bad service. Many American based companies try to reproduce the customer service atmosphere that surrounds their operations in the U.S. when they set up shop in Australia. In many instances though this does not work. For one reason or another, not the least being the slack attitude of the average Australian worker, the facade of American business is often transplanted into Australian society but management cannot faithfully reproduce the philosophies behind these businesses.

There are some exceptions such as Denny's Restaurants. These are a new invention in Australia, so to speak, because they provide medium priced meals in a comfortable environment. Prior to Denny's, one had a choice of pubs that served lunch and dinner at reasonable prices, the local greasy spoon cafe or relatively expensive restaurants if one didn't want take-out, or take-away as it is called in Australia. I know that Denny's is not a four star restaurant but it is a booming success in Australia because of the quality of food and especially the flawless service compared to what Australians are accustomed to. We stayed quite near the first

Australian Denny's on our recent trip and I swear that there was never a time when we drove by that the parking lot and restaurant weren't almost full. More power to them!

The overwhelming feeling one gets after visiting Australia, if one likes good service, is that everything seems just a little out of place. If the traveler can put up with sub-standard service that may cause some minor annoyance during one's stay, there is plenty to recommend a vacation in Australia even for the most veteran American traveler.

THE COST OF LIVING

When it really comes down to it, the cost of living in Australia is relatively higher than in the average U.S. city or town.

My definition of the cost of living is simply the total of those expenses that have to be paid in relation to one's total income. As one can see from the following comparison charts, just about everything one can imagine costs more dollar-for-dollar in Australia than it does in the U.S.

I have deliberately avoided using any exchange rate conversion because Australians buy goods in Australia with Australian dollars, and Americans buy goods in the U.S. with American dollars. It is only tourists that find themselves advantaged or disadvantaged by exchange rates in most cases. Apart from goods and services being relatively more expensive in Australia, jobs generally pay less and are taxed much heavier than their U.S. equivalents. (See Figures 44, 45, 46, &47)

Saturday afternoon shopping NOW

Tired of the hassles of peak hour shopping?
The Saturday morning rush to the shops?
The traffic jam, parking problems, the wait at check-out queues?

What you **need** is Saturday afternoon shopping.
And you're not alone...a recent national survey shows that more than
two of every three Australians want Saturday afternoon shopping.

SATURDAY AFTERNOON SHOPPING WILL GIVE YOU:

- **MORE TIME TO SHOP, ESPECIALLY IF YOU WORK**
- **YOUR WHOLE FAMILY CAN SHOP TOGETHER**
- **COMPETITIVE PRICES FOR A WIDER RANGE OF GOODS**
- **SHOPPING CONVENIENCE WITHOUT EXTRA COST**
- **BETTER CUSTOMER SERVICES**

The time has come to bring Victorian shopping hours more in line with the need
and convenience of the shopping public.

Other benefits — see other side

LET'S GO SATURDAY, ALL THE WAY

Fig 43

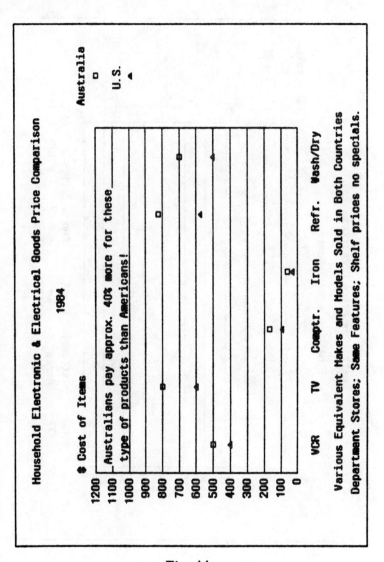

Fig 44

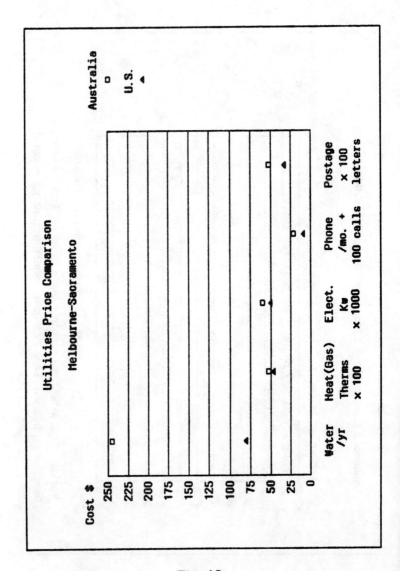

Fig 45

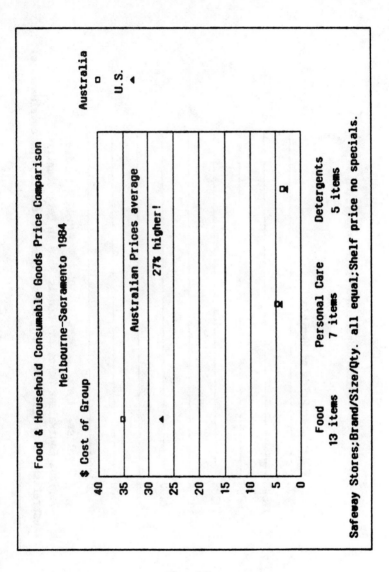

Fig 46

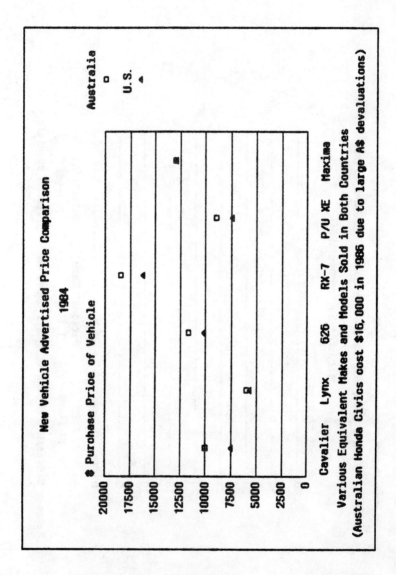

Fig 47

Chapter
Seven

The
Australian
Government
and
its
Effects

THE AUSTRALIAN CONSTITUTION

This somewhat shabby document is a disgrace to its name. When it was compiled and enacted to allow so called independence in 1901, executive power was left in the hands of the British Monarch's appointed Governor General. This was a brilliant exercise to make Australians feel that they were free, but in reality Australia's political status was little changed. The Constitution provides no Bill of Rights or right to vote. The Governor General can actually appoint anyone he likes to run the country, as we saw in 1975 when the Governor General dissolved both federal houses of parliament.

The document supposedly guarantees certain freedoms, but no one is ever read his rights when arrested, because he hasn't really got any rights. The courts are tools of the government in power. There is an overwhelming resistance to change in Australia as evidenced by the handful of constitutional amendments that have been passed in the last 80 years. It is almost guaranteed that any constitutional amendment, and there have been some good ones, is doomed before any referendum is held. The referendum on constitutional matters is, in fact, the only way the Australian people can influence anything between elections. The catch is, the government in power is the only authority able to place referendums before the people. Not only do the people have to vote on referendum matters, but a 2/3 majority of the voters must approve the measure, and a 2/3 majority of the states must also approve the measure. There have been many instances where 75% of the population have approved a referendum, only to be shot down by tiny states, like Tasmania with less than half a million people, who stop the 2/3 state majority from passing it.

The Australian Constitution amounts to very little when judged in the light of guaranteeing people their freedom, fair laws and a prosperous and secure future for their land. (See Figure 48)

THE POLITICAL PARTIES

The major political parties in Australia are The Labor Party, The Liberal Party, The National Party and The Australian Democrats.

The Labor Party, currently in control of the federal government, has its roots firmly planted in the 'working class' people of Australia. The Labor Party has traditionally viewed the political process from a belief that the nation's landed gentry and businesses were out to exploit their employees. This accounts for the Labor Party's firm commitment to government ownership of many business enterprises as a means of redistributing the wealth away from the society's traditional power bases. The only trouble is that it hasn't and continues not to work.

In the past four decades, the Labor Party has only been in power at the federal level about six years. The Labor Party has always been accused of, and rightly so in many instances, of being in the pockets of the extremely powerful Australian trade union movement, and has been painted pink by Australian conservatives for its blatant support of highly socialistic programs. The Labor Party is more radical and socialist oriented than other major political parties and it is so far 'left' in it's outlook that there is no equivalent to it in U.S. politics, unless you delve into the platforms of the Socialist and Communist parties of America.

The Liberal Party has controlled the federal government for most of the past forty years. Its name is something of a contradiction in terms. The

Bill of rights would apply only to Government actions, seminar told

CANBERRA. — An Australian bill of rights would not be incorporated into the Constitution for many years, would not necessarily cover the media, and would protect citizens only from Government actions, the convener of the Attorney-General's task force on the bill said on the weekend.

The bill would not regulate the actions of private individuals and corporations, Ms Gae Pincus, told a Media Law Association of Australasia seminar on freedom of expression.

Fig 48
(Courtesy of The Melbourne Age)

Kerr breaks silence to deny CIA claim

The former Governor-General, Sir John Kerr, has publicly denied that his decision to sack the Whitlam Government in November 1975 was influenced by the US Central Intelligence Agency.

Fig 49
(Courtesy of The Melbourne Age)

party's political outlook is considered conservative in Australia and it always supports the interests of business and the wealthy. It is not liberal in its thinking or policies. If you were looking for an equivalent U.S. political party there is no real comparison outside the radical or 'Leftist' Democrats. It is only Australian Liberal Party ultra–conservatives who call for the sale of government–owned businesses and for a reformation of the tax structures. These enlightened voices in the Australian wilderness are considered as extremely dangerous 'rightists'.

The National Party, a declining force in Australian politics, has its roots in rural Australia. The National Party, once called the Country Party, because it gained much of its strength from farmers throughout the nation, was responsible much of the time for keeping the Liberal Party in power because the two parties formed a coalition at the federal level.

The National Party is more conservative than the Liberal Party so the two groups make good bedfellows. The National Party was, and still is, unashamedly a special interest lobby for farmers and ranchers throughout Australia. The National Party's influence in the past years enabled them to rig the electoral system so that rural electorates could place a member in parliament with about 60% of the vote required in urban electorates. This situation has changed somewhat, but there still remains a rather high 10% electoral variation. An equivalent political power in the U.S. would be the middle–of–the–road democrats from the farm states.

The Australian Democrats are a small but powerful force in Australian politics once were called the Australia Party. This party holds the balance of power in the senate, therefore it can influence legislation to its liking. Its political stance is rather middle–of–the–road compared to the other major parties and it seems to have the general interests of Australia at heart more so than the other major political parties. Moderate U.S. Democrats and moderate U.S Republicans would share much of their outlook with the Australian Democrats.

THE HOUSES OF PARLIAMENT

The federal houses of parliament consist of the House of Representatives, the lower house, and the Senate, the upper house.

The Australian House of Representatives has 148 members. This membership may not seem excessive to the American public, but let me put this in perspective. Australia contains about 16 million people. This means that there is one federal representative for each 101,000 persons. In the U.S. there are approximately 240 million people represented by 435 members of the house of representatives, or one member per 550,000 persons. This means that Australians are over-represented in the lower house by a ratio of more than five to one compared to the U.S. Now look at the Australian Senate that has 76 members, or one per 197,000 persons. The 100 member U.S.Senate has one senator per 2.4 million persons. The Australian Senate ends up being over-represented by a ratio of 12 to one compared to the U.S. In 1983, both Australian houses of parliament voted to increase their membership by 19% to reach these outrageous levels!

It would seem that Australians believe the way to meet insurmountable social and economic problems is to throw more politicians into the governmental process. I believe the feeling is more representation is better representation. I doubt very much this has any basis in fact in the Australian experience.

Not only are the Australian people over-represented in federal government, but the same holds true for the state governments. Take for example Victoria where four million people are represented by 60 assemblymen in the lower house, and 30 councilors in the upper house of state parliament. An assemblyman represents 66,666 people and a councillor represents 133,333 people. Compared to California where 80 assemblymen each represent 294,000 people, and 40 senators each represent 588,000 people. Victorians are over-represented by a ratio of about four and a half to one at the state level compared to California. For all this representation Australians have no fewer problems, nor do their governments come to decisions any more quickly than do the U.S. governments. On the contrary, Australian politics and governmental agencies move with dinosaur-like speed in regards to all manner of public business agenda items.

The important part of this entire argument concerning excessive government and over-representation, which few Australians seem to be aware of, concerns not only the number of representatives but the massive support services that each representative must have to do his job effectively.

If the U.S. were represented at the same rate per 100,000 population as Australians, there would be 2175 members in the house of representatives and 1200 senators! Think about how much it would cost the U.S. taxpayer to support such an establishment. This may explain why Australian taxes are so much higher than their U.S. counterparts.

Based on my experience in living under both systems, I can assure you the American public get much better representation for its political dollar and its representatives are far more accessible and responsive than their Australian counterparts.

WHO REALLY GOVERNS AUSTRALIA?

The party or parties that form the majority in the house of representatives elects its own leader to hold the position of 'Prime Minister'. It is usually the majority party leader who has run, just like any other candidate for the House, to represent an electorate.

However, the prime minister is not the 'Head of State'. That role is filled by the 'Governor General', who is appointed by the monarch of Great Britain to oversee the affairs of Australia. The Governor General's signature must appear on all federal legislative bills, just as the appointed State Governors' signatures must appear on all state laws, before becoming effective. Is this a democracy in comparison to the U.S. experience?

Unlike the U.S. government that has three aspects, The President, The Congress and The Courts, Australia lacks these checks and balances that protect the society from the inroads of the politicians and special interest groups.

To illustrate just who holds the real power take the example of what happened in 1975 when the governor general conspired with the leader of the Liberal Party and the Chief Justice of The Australian High Court to dissolve both houses of the Australian parliament. An equivalent act in the U.S. would be presidential authority to dismiss all members of congress by the stroke of his pen. In other words the Australian people experienced a bloodless coup. The leadership of the nation was then turned over to the leader of the Liberal Party which was in opposition at the time, and the Liberal Party leader played caretaker, so to speak, until elections were held a month or so later. This entire episode was subsequently shown to be a conspiracy that was illegal in the spirit of the

Party first

Congratulations to the nine Labor women MPs condemning Mrs Sibree. They prove what we all suspected; an ALP MP's first loyalty is to the party and not the electorate where it should be.

PETER GOMPERTZ,
Yarra Glen.

Fig 50
(Courtesy of The Melbourne Age)

Voting to avoid a fine

from J. M. Gascoigne

I have just exercised my democratic right to engage in a pointless
exercise. On Saturday I voted not
for the municipal council candidate of my choice but to avoid
prosecution. It is my guess that I
was among a considerable majority so motivated.

Fig 51
(Courtesy of The Melbourne Age)

constitution, but the Australian political system lacks the independent power to bring the perpetrators of this injustice to trial. (See Figure 49)

The ultimate power in Australia is held by the governor general even though the power inside the parliament is held by the prime minister as the leader of the majority party.

In addition to the power of the leader of the majority party, more power is gained by the parliamentary rules that allow only the majority party to introduce legislation during any session, unless the majority party gives special dispensation to an opposition member to introduce a bill, a proposal that the majority would support anyway.

Because of similar basic party rules adopted by both the Liberal and Labor parties, politicians in Australia have a strange sense of loyalty. An Australian politician votes and makes decisions according to his political party's dictates first, supports the interests of the country second, for his own self interest third, for the special interest lobbies that supported his campaign fourth, and lastly for the citizens in the electorate that put him in office. An American politician usually votes first for the citizens and special interests in the electorate, second for his country, third for his own self interest and finally for his political party's interests. (See Figure 50)

The party rules that foster these strange priorities of Australian politicians are quite simple. If a candidate is voted into office as a Labor or Liberal candidate and votes against the party's directive, he is thrown out of the party and has to work as an independent. There is absolutely no hope of his future endorsement by the party machine.

There are rare occasions when laws come to vote that allow 'conscience votes' by all members without threat of reprisal. Thus most votes in parliament are perfectly predictable along party lines everytime, especially when the politicians' political life is at stake on each vote.

The way this unbelievable political power can be used has been demonstrated many times. It literally means that any government that comes to power can change any law to suit itself, and often does.

In one case of blatant abuse of this political power, I heard a past prime minister say on national television that if a particular cabinet minister of his was found guilty of fraud and forgery, his government would change that part of the appropriate corporate law and make it retroactive to assure that the colleague was not found guilty. What kind of respect can Australian politicians expect the public to have for the laws of the land when they act like that?

The next burning question that may come to mind is, 'Why does everyone in Australia let them get away with all this?' The simple explanation is that there is nothing anyone can do about it.

Once representatives are elected to office, they are there for three years in the house of representatives or six years in the senate; there is nothing the electorate can do about removing them unless perchance a representative is sent to jail for a felony. Australia has no effective petition or initiative system that allows the public to vent its displeasure or express its desires between elections. Even if every voter placed his signature on a petition to the federal government, the only obligation the government has is to read the petition in the House and then it can be trash canned. Without access to a petition or initiative procedure, the Australian public are actually prisoners of their own vote if politicians fail to act in accordance to their general promises.

That is the way government power works in Australia. Compared to the U.S., it is far from a checks and balances system as practiced in this country. Unfortunately, there appears to be no real change in the wind.

THE VOTING SYSTEM

What you are about to read is probably beyond anything you have ever imagined.

To start with, it is the law that everyone of voting age MUST VOTE or BE FINED! That's right, vote or receive a fine of $20 for not exercising a citizen's democratic duty. Is it no wonder Australian spokesmen brag about the almost universal voter turnout at federal and state elections with laws like that on the books. Some people believe that an election is more valid if everyone turns out to vote, even though some may be participating only to avoid a monetary penalty. (See Figure 51)

The next part of the voting story concerns how votes are cast. Ballots are hand marked with pencil in Australia, much the same way union election ballots are completed in this country. Almost universally throughout Australia the ballot is a printed sheet with the candidates listed in alphabetical order from top to bottom. There are no political party identifying marks against any name on the ballot. One has to be familiar with the name of one's candidate before seeing the ballot if you want to vote for a particular political party.

To top off this compulsory and apparently confusing system, the voter doesn't just place a mark in the box next to the preferred candidates name. He or she must place a '1' in the box next to the preferred candidate. If there are 7 people on the ballot, you must mark the remaining six '2' to '7'. This is called preferential voting for those who are unfamiliar with this bizarre process. Not only must the voter place a number beside each name, but he cannot miss a number or repeat one, otherwise the entire ballot is considered invalid and will not be counted. Also if any other mark of any kind is made on the ballot paper, the ballot will be invalidated immediately! The logic behind this system is that if there is no clear 50%+ winner on the first choice count, the electoral office then counts the second choices as though they were first choices and so on, until a clear winner is decided. This avoids the run-off election that takes place in the U.S. from the two top vote receivers.

Unfortunately for Australia, this particularly strange system often ends up putting candidates into office who are disliked by a majority of the electorate. This system of voting allowed the Liberal/National coalition to rule for many years, even though the Labor party could poll more first preference votes than the coalition. The height of stupidity about preferential voting is revealed when it comes to federal senate election ballots. As ten senators are selected from each Australian state, there may be in excess of 50 names on the ballot from which to chose. The same preferential voting system applies to these long lists. In the 1980 federal senate elections, the ballots were so complicated, causing vast numbers to be invalidated, it was as though no one in Western Australia bothered to go to the polls. (See Figure 52)

Some states have changed the ballot laws to allow optional preferential voting for state elections, and the names on the ballot are now juggled around and not in alphabetical order. This is a far-sighted act in

Australian electoral procedures. The main problem with candidates being listed in alphabetical order on a ballot is the 'donkey' vote as it's known. As people are in violation of the law if they don't vote, many appear at the polling booth and write 1 thru whatever straight down the ballot, regardless of who the candidates are, to avoid that monetary penalty for failing to exercise one's political rights. It is a political fact of life in Australia that most candidates have a better chance of being elected to office if his or her name starts with A-E, because of the advantage gained by the donkey vote.

An analysis of this voting system brings me to the conclusion that the individual is not only forced to vote in Australia against his will if he is not interested in the political process under threat of monetary penalty, but when he does vote, the preferential voting system actually forces him to vote for people he would never consider putting in office. This is a poor excuse for an electoral process in the 1980's. One would expect to find such a bizarre voting system in a banana republic, not Australia!

THE MOVEMENT FOR INDEPENDENCE

There is a movement in Australia to cut all ties with Great Britain, to throw out the old constitution, to create a new constitution complete with a Bill of Rights and to get on with creation of an independent nation in the 1980's.

Many conservative Australians and loyal Britons view this as treasonous because they desire that Australia always be identified with Great Britain and all that she stands for. In my estimation, by the year 2001, Australia will have drafted a new constitution and will gracefully withdraw from British influence the way Canada did recently. In any event, Great Britain will have no choice in the matter, except to gracefully accept the situation and wish Australia good luck on her merry way.

RESISTANCE TO CHANGE IN AUSTRALIA

One of Australia's greatest handicaps has been its stodgy British methods of resisting change in the name of good form.

Change to the average Australian is something almost evil. The 'don't rock the boat' attitude is far ahead of any other national motto. The resistance to change runs so deep, in fact, that Australia is hemorrhaging at the thought of computers entering everyday life in Australia. For instance, there was only one manufacturer of modems (the devices that allow computers to communicate with each other over telephone lines), that was approved for use in Australia in 1984. Compare this to the U.S. where literally hundreds of brands of modems are approved for everyday use. Are they afraid of damaging their telephone lines with other brands?

The fact that so many Australians have British and Southern European backgrounds also adds to this apparent need to resist change. These people come from old countries, with old ideas, and they wish to impart this conservatism to their new land and to their Australian–born children. This myopic resistance to change must give way at some stage if Australia is to forge ahead as a nation with the rest of the western world.

FROM WHOM CAN AUSTRALIA LEARN?

If the people of Australian weren't so irrationally anti–American government, business and institutions, they would see that Australia could do itself a favor by becoming more realistic about what America has to offer and its potential future. They would also realize that they can't follow the British way of doing things and expect to have a great and prosperous nation, something that most all Australians expect their destiny to be, ready to adapt to the future economic challenges that will face all western nations.

Before Australia can become a fully fledged independent nation, it must look at the U.S. economic and political systems, and model Australia's future on many of these practical and viable ways of coping with a modern industrialized nation.

Fig 52
(Courtesy of The Melbourne Age)

Chapter Eight

Social Security and the Safety Net

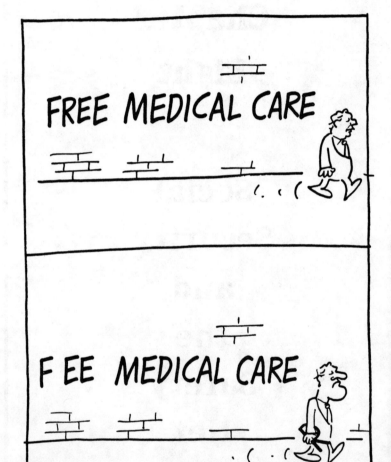

RETIREMENT BENEFITS

Australia's social security system is similar to that in the U.S. But, the Australian system is different enough to raise serious questions about how much security there really is.

Unlike the U.S., there is no separate deduction on the pay check stub for a social security payment. Part of the one-item tax bite is for distribution to the retirement pension for Australians. To qualify a man must be 65 years old (or 60 for veterans of foreign wars), and a woman must be 60 years old.

In May 1984, according to the Australian Department of Social Security, the Age Pension pays A$384.42 a month for single persons, and A$641.12 a month for married couples. In comparison, according to the U.S. Social Security Administration as of April 1984, the average age pension payment to each retired worker was US$442.00 per month. An Australian retired married couple can earn no more than A$1497.26 per month from other sources before their pension is eliminated, and a single can only earn A$897.84 per month from other sources before his pension is eliminated. These limits are raised to A$2169.78 per month for married couples, and A$1302.47 per month for singles after the age of 70. There is more or less free medical care for age pension recipients, similar to the Medicare coverage here in the U.S. The Australian medical coverage requires less in the way of co-payments than U.S. Medicare.

Companies are not obliged to provide retirement plans for their employees, but many jobs in the private sector, and all government related jobs which make up 27% of the work force, provide for Superannuation fund contributions. These provide benefits similar to the average U.S. company and government retirement programs. The income derived from these plans, as well as whole life insurance policy payouts, will reduce the retiree's age pension payments.

Recently the Australian federal government instituted a despicable program for individuals who withdraw their retirement funds in one lump sum. Money contributed to superannuation funds is taxed before it is deposited, and the government now taxes lump sum withdrawals at retirement at 30%! This amounts to double taxation on retirement contributions.

Age Pensioners receive discounts on drugs, electricity, heating gas, train travel within their own state, car registration and property taxes. While these benefits range from 10%-50%, they hardly offset the severe income limitations and the tax liabilities one may readily face at retirement.

An individual must generally have lived in Australia for 10 years prior to applying for the age pension, but there is no requirement that he must have worked and contributed taxes to pay for his retirement benefits.

Many immigrants found that they could take up residence in Australia, be joined by their aged parents whom they support for 10 years who then automatically become eligible for the age pension. Activities like this add to the growing burden of taxation on everyone.

SICKNESS BENEFITS

Long term disability coverage is payable to anyone who is unable to work because of accident or an extended illness.

To qualify the recipient must have been a resident of Australia for the past 12 months, or, and this is quite amazing, file a declaration stating that he intends to live permanently in Australia.

When I immigrated to the U.S., my wife and her family had to guarantee that they would take care of me if I was unable to work. As a voluntary immigrant, I could not qualify for Social Security or welfare benefits without first working for a period of time. According to the Australian Department of Social Security as of May 1984, Sickness Benefits pay A$193.50 per month for singles under 18, A$384.42 per month for singles 18 and over, and A$641.13 per month for married couples. These benefits are reduced of course by the receipt of other income and are eliminated for married couples receiving A$834.63 per month income from other sources.

INVALID/DISABLED PENSION

Those persons permanently blind or permanently medically unfit for work can qualify for an Invalid Pension. There is no minimum length of residency in Australia for those persons who become blind or disabled while in Australia. According to the Australian Department of Social Security in May 1984, the benefits and extra income limitations are almost identical to that of the age pension, A$384.42 for singles and A$641.12 for married couples. In comparison, the average payment for U.S. disabled workers in April 1984 according to the U.S. Social Security Administration, was US$455.00 per month.

WIDOW'S PENSION

The widow's pension is payable to a widow with a) at least one child under 16 years of age, or a dependent full-time student over 16 but under 25, b) to a widow aged 50 or more with no children, or c) to a widow in a) but 45 or older when the last child leaves her care. According to the Australian Department of

Social Security as of May 1984, the widow's pension paid A$384.42 per month to a recipient without children, A$470.42 per month with one child, and A$522.02 per month with two children. In comparison, the U.S. Social Security Administration as of April 1984 provided 3/4 of the value of the deceased's full retirement benefit for each child under 18.

SUPPORTING PARENTS BENEFITS

Any parent separated, divorced or unmarried, can qualify to be supported by the government at a rate of A$470.40 per month with one child, and A$522.02 per month with two children. The usual restrictions on other income also apply. This is one benefit of which I have personal knowledge of blatant abuse.

Friends of ours in Melbourne had a young nephew in Canberra, Australia's capital, married with one toddler and a very pregnant wife. He decided he needed to take some time off for work for an extended vacation as he had worked in one position for the eternity of one whole year. Formulating a vacation itinerary, he declared that he wanted to 'see' Australia. Ignoring his wife's protests about minor considerations like their mere existence, he decided to take his child and hitchhike across Australia. Of course there were to be regular drop-ins to "mooch off" relatives on the way.

When he departed Canberra, his wife immediately applied for a Supporting Parent's Benefit because her husband had left her. The husband, with toddler in tow, arrived in Melbourne and applied for his Supporting Parent's Benefit because he was separated from his wife. The Australian government thereby gladly, albeit unknowingly, paid this one family A$940.84 per month so that the pregnant wife could stay at home, while the 'bread winner', so to speak,

102

travelled around Australia at the tax payers expense. I was just informed recently that this couple were doing this very thing once again at the end of 1986. What other country in the world can offer young families such benefits? It is no wonder a whole generation of young Australians is growing up with the attitude that the world owes them a living.

UNEMPLOYMENT BENEFITS

Here is the one benefit that will most amaze the average American. These benefits apply to all those people temporarily out of work, who are willing to work and are looking for work.

Does this sound pretty much the same as the U.S.? The social travesty surrounding the Australian unemployment system is that one does not need to have worked a day in his life to be eligible to collect unemployment benefits! Any person, 16 years or older who leaves school and cannot find work within six weeks, is eligible to draw unemployment benefits, a practice associated with little social stigma. On the other hand, most Americans think that their unemployed youth are lazy or are unemployed because they haven't properly prepared themselves for employment.

Benefits range from A$193.50 per month for those under 18 to A$641.13 per month for married couples. The usual income from other sources restrictions apply to the unemployment benefit. In comparison, the U.S. Department of Labor in 1982 gave the average unemployment insurance benefit payment as US$513.16 per month.

MEDICINE AND HEALTHCARE

Prior to 1973, Australia operated under a medical insurance philosophy of 'Have medical insurance or pay the bills yourself!' The vast majority of jobs in Australia did not (and still don't) provide medical insurance as one of the benefits, so in 1973 under a new government, a national healthcare program known as Medibank was created.

Medical care was not nationalized, as most hospitals were already government-owned or supported, but instead a system of government subsidies for medical costs was created. The government would refund approximately 85% of all medical costs incurred by patients. This was welcome as the average man no longer had to fear illness if he could not afford private health insurance. As basic hospital services were covered by the national health system, the private health insurance business moved into the area of private hospital room accommodations and elective surgery coverage. A very profitable arrangement indeed.

Meanwhile, doctors, specialists, surgeons, and other medical providers were now mostly released from having to worry about bad debts, and in fact if they accepted the governments 85% coverage level for services, they no longer needed to chase any patients for unpaid bills. This national healthcare system worked to most people's satisfaction and suffered very little abuse from over use by patients or fraudulent billing by medical providers.

It was studied on the basis of cost and efficiency by the government during its first year of operation. In its second year of operation the public was forced to help pay the cost of the service by being subject to modest new income tax levies payable at tax refund time. If one was single, marking the appropriate box on the tax return meant that one received about $70 less in refund, and if one were married it would cost about $150 of your tax refund.

This was a fine example of the painless extraction of cash to pay for the national health system. A contentious point was that the individual paid through his taxes even though he may also have purchased private health insurance. Medibank was the most efficient national health program in the world, with administrative costs of only 5%. Where is Medibank today? Subsequent governments of opposing philosophies gained power and methodically dismantled Medibank while telling the Australian people they would maintain and improve it!

Today Australian Medicare is in place of Medibank, a system purported to be excellent by the government but decried by most as a sham compared to the original Medibank. What do these benefits really mean?

Australia has always been perceived as offering more in the way of retirement security than the U.S. This is extremely doubtful, especially when one takes into consideration the draconian taxation structure that burdens one from the cradle to grave in Australia. Recently, recipients of old age pensions have been subjected to 'asset tests' to determine if they were too wealthy in assets, regardless of real income, to be receiving their age pension! One thing is certain. The U.S. economic system allows a person to work hard and accumulate retirement benefits and income far in excess of what is possible in Australia, especially in view of how much you get to keep after taxes in the U.S..

Chapter
Nine

Taxes

FEDERAL TAXES

INCOME TAX

If the reader had imagined Australia as some sort of low or no tax haven on the other side of paradise, I am sorry but he is about to be bitterly disappointed.

To call Australia anything less than a high tax country compared to the U.S. would be outright false. The Australian government and press have a nasty habit of always telling the Australian population that they are a low tax country when compared to Europe! Australian spokesmen somehow forget that the U.S. exists when it comes to comparing tax systems.

Income tax, Pay As You Earn (PAYE), is represented on the paycheck as a single figure. There is no provision or separation of Social Security, Unemployment and Disability, or how much the state receives from the lump sum. The reason for this I feel is that unlike the U.S., there exists only one general revenue fund in the federal government which funds all government paid benefits. By not having separate Social Security, Unemployment, Disability, and State Taxes, the Australian government has been able to rob the people blind for years. Without separate accounts there is no guarantee that the government has the money or long term fiscal capacity to provide benefits on a long term basis. Another reason for not having separate accounts, is that at any time in the future the government can raise general taxes for whatever purpose it sees fit, without having to justify it to anybody.

At first observation, Australia's tax code may appear very appealing, and actually give the impression that Australians pay far less tax than Americans. This may be the case at very low income levels, but it certainly does not apply when all factors, including tax deductions and sales taxes are taken into consideration.

At very low income levels the Australian federal PAYE starts at 25% for each dollar earned in excess of A$4596; up until A$4596 there is no tax payable. This is a great advantage when compared to the U.S. PAYE rate of 19.41% at US$4596. (The U.S. PAYE rate quoted consists of 11% Federal, 6.8% Social Security, .1% Disability and 1.6% Cal. State.)

At a higher income level of say $12,500, the Australian PAYE rate is 16.8% compared to the U.S. PAYE rate, all taxes combined, of 18.45%! This still looks good for the Australian taxpayer.

If $19,500 is the third income level we look at, the Australian PAYE is 21.9%, compared to a combined U.S. PAYE rate of 22.31%. It still looks good for the Australians but notice that the gap is closing.

Australian PAYE on $28,000 is 29.5%. The U.S. combined rate is 27.52%! Ah, ha! What is happening? Could it possibly be that at this income level the American's actual pay a lower initial tax rate? Read on and discover more.

33.42% at $35,000 is the Australian PAYE rate, where all honest American tax payers will only shell out 27.9%!

Getting into the real money, so to speak, $50,000 a year in Australia attracts a PAYE rate of 41.69%!!! The U.S. PAYE combined rate is only 32.51%!

Taking into consideration that both Australia and America now have more than 50% of all households with two incomes, most families in both countries earn roughly $30,000 – $50,000 per year.

Why do I claim that Australia is subject to much higher income taxes? After studying the tax deductions and credits of both tax systems, one can really appreciate how the Australian people are burdened by their tax system. The Tax Comparison Table of family incomes from $12,500 to $50,000, which includes various allowable deductions and credits, clearly shows excessive Australian tax rates compared to those in the U.S. (See Figure 53)

Australia's close neighbor, New Zealand, exacts 60% PAYE taxes for every dollar earned over $22,001 per year!

At the lower end of the income scale, Australians actually pay less tax than their American counterparts. But at the level of $28,000, an Australian family pays 22% more in taxes than Americans of the same income level. At $50,000, the Australians are bled an additional 106% in taxes than Americans. Are there any Americans out there still complaining about U.S. taxes?

So far remember, we have only been talking about PAYE income taxes, that are deducted directly from the pay check. Other forms of taxes, like sales, import, excise and city taxes play a big part in determining just how highly taxed a country is. (See Figure 54)

SALES TAXES

The federal government of Australia collects sales taxes and then disburses revenues to the state governments. This simple arrangement allows one to see that Australia has a very centralized government. Sales taxes are a very complex area for the Australian bureaucracy to handle.

In the true British tradition of narrow minded and 19th century administrative procedures, Australia does not have a flat sales tax rate as exists in most states of the U.S. On the contrary, the Australian sales tax varies depending on whether items are classified as 'essentials', such as food, or 'luxuries', such as shaving cream and razors! Food is not taxed, so there is one shared tax level between Australia and America albeit a no-tax level.

But that is where the equivalence ends. The following goods are included in the 7.5% sales tax rate:

Household Furniture, Drapes, Carpets, Airconditioners, Dishwashers, Hand Tools, Garage Tools and Handkerchiefs.

The following big ticket item attracts a 15% sales tax: Automobiles!

This partial list of "luxury" items attract the hefty rate of 32.5% sales tax:

Jewelry, except wedding rings, Badges, Knives, Silverware, Pens, Watches and Clocks, Shampoos and Conditioners for hair, Cosmetics, Hair Brushes, Photographic Film and Equipment, Record and Tape Players, Blank and Pre-recorded Tapes, TV's and VCR's.

Can you imagine spending 32.5% of each dollar on tax the next time you go out and buy a TV or VCR? Why aren't Australians as mad as hell about this gouging of their disposable income?

Apart from the fact that they have been thoroughly brainwashed for the past 20 years and numbed into the belief that these high taxes are necessary, the sales tax is NEVER displayed as a separate item or

110

THE NEW TAX BRACKETS

Annual Taxable income $	Tax payable
0 to 4595	Nil
4596 to 12,500	Nil + 25c for each $1 in excess of $4595
12,501 to 19,500	$1976.25 + 30c for each $1 in excess of $12,500
19,501 to 28,000	$4076.25 + 46c for each $1 in excess of $19,500
28,001 to 35,000	$7986.25 + 48c for each $1 in excess of $28,000
35,001 and over	$11,346.25 + 60c for each $1 in excess of $35,000

THE OLD BRACKETS

0 to 4595	Nil
4596 to 19,500	Nil + 30c for each $1 in excess of $4595
19,501 to 35,788	$4471.50 + 46c for each $1 in excess of $19,500
35,789 and over	$11,963.98 + 60c for each $1 in excess of $35,788

Fig 53
(Courtesy of The Melbourne Age)

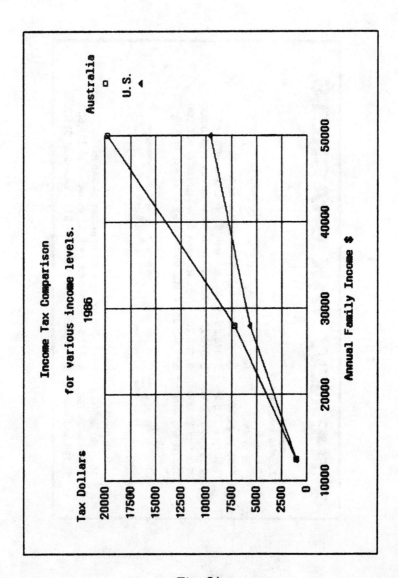

Fig 54

any price tag. It is built right into the price on the shelf and the shopper pays what is rung on the cash register.

I really believe that the Australian business world would do itself and the Australian people a service if every item was ticketed with the retail price and the sales tax stated separately. I believe that there would be a national outcry and a tumbling of tax rates within a short time if this policy was adopted.

Needless to say, sales taxes, no matter how much one pays in any one year, are NOT tax deductible on personal tax returns. Compared to Americans, Australians are burdened by an absolutely enormous sales tax bill as well as a significantly higher personal income tax bill. (See Figure 55)

GASOLINE TAXES

The Australian federal government levies taxes on gasoline. At the gas pump, more than 50% of the price paid is tax. To begin with, gas is over priced, 54+ cents per liter or $2.20+/gallon in August 1986, because the government allows the oil companies to charge what Saudi Arabia receives for its crude, regardless of the cost of production or the free market forces in Australia. Even with the current crash of oil prices, the Australian government increased taxes to keep the retail price of gasoline stable! The Australian motorist rarely experiences long term reductions in the price of gasoline as a result of driving less, or because of a surplus of the commodity; unlike here in California, where motorists can still buy a gallon of gas for 60 cents less than when my wife and I arrived in 1981.

IMPORT DUTIES AND EXCISE

Here is where I hope to lay to its final rest the myth that the protection of native industry saves jobs and is ultimately better for the consumer and the economy at large.

The Australian government has practiced a long history of protectionism and the population pays dearly for the government privilege of raking off billions per year to finance its hopelessly antiquated, inefficient and ineffective programs. Australian protectionism levies are between 15% and 150% of the value of the goods landed in Australia. This is bloody piracy on the high seas no matter how such draconian activities are justified. It just doesn't mean for instance, that autos that arrive completely manufactured are stuck with a duty of 90% at the docks, but cars that are manufactured in Australia, have this extra cost for imports built into their prices. No domestic car manufacturer in his right mind is going to sell equivalent models $1000's cheaper than the foreign made imports. The Australian consumer pays this extra mark-up that the imports have to bear when they buy ANY car!

There is also the economic myth that thousands of jobs are being saved by imposing these high import duties. I strongly suggest that an open door trading policy, combined with an overhaul of the infrastructure, free capital investment and open immigration policies, would turn Australia into a world industrial giant and allow the country to mature, out from under the burden of its British legacy, that of an agricultural/resource based economy.

Such an approach would do far more for providing Australian jobs and protecting the economy than any amount of import taxes. There has been some small

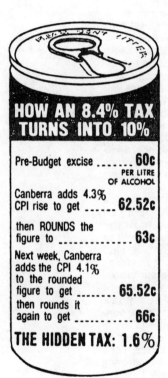

HOW AN 8.4% TAX TURNS INTO 10%

Pre-Budget excise **60c**
PER LITRE
OF ALCOHOL

Canberra adds 4.3%
CPI rise to get **62.52c**

then ROUNDS the
figure to **63c**

Next week, Canberra
adds the CPI 4.1%
to the rounded
figure to get **65.52c**
then rounds it
again to get **66c**

THE HIDDEN TAX: 1.6%

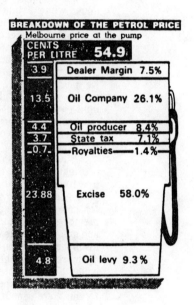

BREAKDOWN OF THE PETROL PRICE
Melbourne price at the pump

CENTS PER LITRE **54.9**

3.9	Dealer Margin	7.5%
13.5	Oil Company	26.1%
4.4	Oil producer	8.4%
3.7	State tax	7.1%
0.7	Royalties	1.4%
23.88	Excise	58.0%
4.8	Oil levy	9.3%

Fig 55
(Courtesy of The Melbourne Age)

Death's duty

Many of your readers will applaud Claude Forell for The Forgotten Cry of Poverty ('The Age', 1/8). It and Canon Hollingworth's Open Letter to the Prime Minister and Archbishop Penman's letter (31/7) are expressions of disillusion with the political process which is shared by many.

With a Labor Government with a huge majority in the Lower House, with a Prime Minister with record popularity, it was natural for people to expect more progress than we have seen towards improving the position of the underprivileged in this society. Instead we have seen each plan to redistribute wealth, in no matter how mild a way, abandoned or emasculated as soon as it meets opposition and seems likely to be an electoral handicap.

It is heartening that churchmen are taking sides with the underprivileged, because basically poverty is a moral issue, a problem for conscience. Regretfully most members of this, the most greedy and materialistic generation in our history, are not prone to be swayed by moral argument, at any rate while they live. After death, however, one might expect it to be different; there seems to be nothing more absurd than carrying one's greed to the grave by opposing death duties on deceased estates.

If the voluntary surrender of privilege and wealth during life is too much to ask of us, death duties are a means of appeasing the conscience without really costing us anything.

Fig 56
(Courtesy of The Melbourne Age)

progress in the past few years in the gradual reduction of import duties, but until import duties are substantially reduced and/or eliminated, such minor adjustments only pay lip service to the changes desired by Australians who truly believe in a free enterprise system.

DEATH TAXES

For all intents and purposes, as in the U.S., there are ways of avoiding death taxes by way of trusts and other useful structures to protect family wealth from the hands of the government. Therefore little comment is required and this should suffice, although some people disagree.(See Figure 56)

DEPARTURE TAX

No, this is not another slick term for death taxes, but a fee that every traveler, citizen or not, must pay before he or she leaves Australia.

Conceived as a way of helping pay the high price of running the international airports that are owned and operated by the federal government, the bureaucrats created this brilliant and lucrative tax. It was also supposed to help compensate for the fact that so many Australians vacation overseas. The Australian government was determined to get at least some of the Australian peoples' vacation dollar.

At its inception, it was no minor fee, $10, unlike the small amount paid in the U.S. by outbound travelers of $3.25 for passport and customs costs. Granted, there are nowhere near the number of travelers departing Australia as the U.S., so Australia made the levy more productive, and because no one can object to any new tax in Australia, it was introduced at that outrageous level of $10 per head! Soon thereafter, little revenue collection booths appeared at the international airports, where every outward bound passenger had to pay $10 to have the official departure tax stamp affixed to his passport before he could leave. Two years later, it was discovered that it was costing a small fortune to have highly paid public servants sitting in these little booths earning all sorts of penalty rates for nights and weekends, collecting these fees. In fact, the cost of collection exceeded the revenues collected. Needless to say, in the true 'Tax 'em to Death' British and Australian tradition, the tax was raised to $20 to cover the high costs of collection.

Be prepared when you visit Australia to have $20 in cash per member of your family when you check into the airport for departure, or you might stay longer than you planned. By the way, they don't take American Express as far as I know.

TOILET SEAT TAXES

This is just a humorous diversion into what the twilight zone of Australian tax collecting could look like.

It was actually proposed some years ago, that to raise more tax revenues in Australia's capital, Canberra, the number of toilets in homes should be used as the base for evaluating this new tax liability. Needless to say, this tax of bodily function support hardware was not adopted. The most important point however, is to consider what type of sick and dangerous bureaucratic mind came up with such a proposal. (See Figure 57)

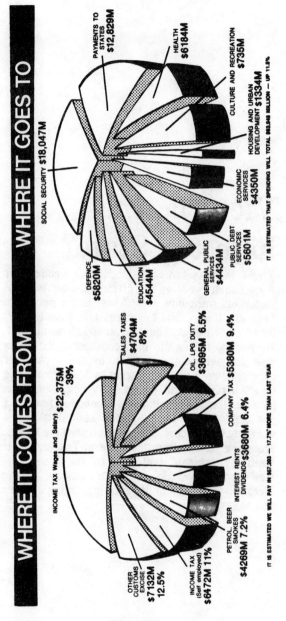

WHERE IT COMES FROM

INCOME TAX (Wages and Salary) $22,375M 39%

OTHER CUSTOMS EXCISE $7132M 12.5%

INCOME TAX (Self employed) $6472M 11%

PETROL, BEER SMOKES $4269M 7.2%

INTEREST RENTS DIVIDENDS $3680M 6.4%

COMPANY TAX $5380M 9.4%

OIL, LPG DUTY $3695M 6.5%

SALES TAXES $4704M 8%

IT IS ESTIMATED WE WILL PAY IN $57,203 — 17.7% MORE THAN LAST YEAR

WHERE IT GOES TO

SOCIAL SECURITY $18,047M

PAYMENTS TO STATES $12,829M

HEALTH $6184M

CULTURE AND RECREATION $735M

HOUSING AND URBAN DEVELOPMENT $1334M

ECONOMIC SERVICES $4350M

PUBLIC DEBT SERVICES $5601M

GENERAL PUBLIC SERVICES $4434M

EDUCATION $4544M

DEFENCE $5820M

IT IS ESTIMATED THAT SPENDING WILL TOTAL $63,849 MILLION — UP 11.5%

Fig 57
(Courtesy of The Melbourne Age)

Victoria, the high tax State?

LAST Monday the State Opposition Leader, Mr Kennett, went on the offensive, claiming that Victorians were now the highest taxed people in Australia. It may have been prescience; but the CPI figures, released on Thursday, tend to bear him out. They show that while the consumer price index rose 2.4 per cent nationally in the September quarter, it rose by 2.9 per cent in Melbourne. The inflation rate for all Australia (which, of course, includes the high Melbourne component) was 8.6 per cent. But in the Victorian capital it was a worrying 9.9 per cent. The publication of the figures brought a rebuke from the Federal Treasurer, Mr Keating, who said that part of the blame for Melbourne's position was attributable to the Victorian Government itself for increasing charges and taxes.

Fig 58
(Courtesy of The Melbourne Age)

STATE TAXES

INCOME TAX

Although it does not appear on the paycheck as a deduction, the state government gets a share of the federal PAYE income tax deduction. It is distributed to the state under a very complex and ultimately inequitable formula that everyone complains about but never does anything to correct. (See Figure 58)

GASOLINE TAX

Again, some of the pump price for gas includes direct state taxes, similar to those collected by the state governments in the United States for road and highway construction and maintenance.

DEATH TAXES

The State of Victoria abolished death duties on 1/1/84. This brought Victoria in line with most other states of Australia.

PAYROLL TAXES

In Victoria, the state government charges employers 6% direct tax on the total value of the business's payroll! That's right, they tax businesses for hiring people. The more people one hires, the more one is taxed on the business's total payroll, this is in addition to the corporate taxes the business pays and in contrast to the 3.6% the California government charges to cover unemployment insurance.

As payroll taxes do not rate as an encouragement to create new jobs in Victorian industry, this leaves the average employer in somewhat of a bind, due the nature of the average Australian worker. Under these conditions, it is not in the best interests of the employer to hire too many people because he gets taxed higher the more employees he has. An employer might then attempt to get his existing workers to work harder and be more productive to cope with increasing business and higher demand.

Now this is not the strong point of the Australian worker. I am not saying the Australian worker wouldn't work in an artificial lung, but productivity for union members, more than 50% of the work force, has never been a strong point. The old adage of 'job preservation', by working slow and at less than peak efficiency, means most businesses have a difficult time reaching peak efficiency. The employer must get the work done so he hires more people, who usually must become union members, and he then has more inefficient workers on staff and he pays higher taxes.

This is reverse economic thinking at its best, but typical of the way Australia deals with its economy!

GIFT TAXES

Like in the U.S., the Australian taxation system views giving money away as another opportunity to share in the transaction. The rates run from 0% on gifts under $50,000 to 22% on amounts over $201,777.

CITY TAXES

These come in the form of property taxes based on improved and unimproved land values. In Victoria in 1984 these taxes ranged from .357% at $44,275 to 1% at $227,700. The city taxes don't stop here though. Water and Sewage rates are extra and can amount to $200-$300 per year. No city taxes are tax-deductible.

BUSINESS TAXES

Australia has more or less the same system as the U.S. of giving attractive tax incentives to business.

Corporations fare fairly well in Australia, especially if they are foreign owned. Up until recently, Australia had a long standing policy that foreign capital was really only allowed into Australia if a business came with it. For example, until two years ago foreign banks and foreign venture capitalists were excluded from the Australian economy, I suspect because they might compete successfully with the established traditional Australian cash sources, so the government limited foreign participation to be in the form of multinational corporations. If a company wanted to invest in Australia they had to create manufacturing and distribution systems within Australia, thus creating jobs and introducing technology capacity to Australia.

Britain, The U.S. and Japan are well represented in the multinational corporate life of Australia. The Australian government, while adopting policies to promote jobs and technology transfer to Australia, had to offer something in return to the multinational corporations. They did this in the form of fantastic tax breaks for these corporations. These corporations have long been able to export the vast majority of their earnings without one penny of federal or state taxes being levied against it.

Billions and billions of dollars have been exported from Australia to invest in other economies because Australia didn't have an attractive and active enough free economy to keep this money in Australia.

The standard corporate tax rate for public and private companies is 49% on every dollar of net income! How does that grab you executives? Compare that robbery with 15%–40% under $100,000 to 46% at $100,000+ in the U.S.! Of course most corporations don't pay taxes, but having almost half one's net earnings evaporate in taxes is enough to consider whether it is even worth being in business as a domestically owned corporation. (See Figure 59)

One problem though with the entire business system in Australia, is that taxes are added at each stage of the manufacturing process. From raw material to finished product, sales taxes of varying percentage are levied each time the product moves to the next stage of the chain. Adding a few percent at each stage may sound harmless, but considering that a product may change hands 5 or 6 times before it is ready for sale, a major added expense is incurred. The Australian government is famous for using the 'a little bit at a time won't hurt anybody' taxation theory.

SMALL BUSINESS TAXES

The small business man in Australia probably has a somewhat easier time when it comes to taxes than the average working person or the corporation for that matter. Except for the problem of having to pay wholesale tax for everything he gets from his supplier if he is manufacturer, prior to him even selling the item, the little businessman can hide income and cheat the tax system just like many businessmen do in America. I must admit though, there seems to be more reason to avoid business taxes in Australia than there does on this side of the Pacific. Successful and honest small businessmen and farmers, as here in the U.S., pay little or no taxes. The average working stiffs of the middle class have to support everybody in Australia as they do in the U.S.

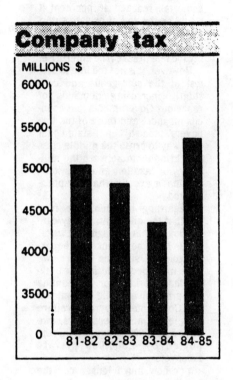

Fig 59
(Courtesy of The Melbourne Age)

Taxing thoughts

from Dr J.H.G. Dyson-Firth

Karl Marx stated that when income tax reached 40 per cent it would be the end of private enterprise or capitalism. We have now passed that point, and it is probably too late to save free enterprise.

However, it is *not* too late to protest at the outrageous and *constantly increasing* demands of rapacious Governments and councils for more and more of the taxpayers' money. Lenin stated that "the way to crush the middle class is to grind them between the millstones of taxation and inflation", and that is *exactly* what is happening today.

Regarding inflation, one may say that the one thing money cannot buy is what it bought last week.

We have now reached the extraordinary situation where we have more people *voting* for a living than working for it. Counting non-productive public servants on the Government payroll, welfare recipients, and pensioners, we have 5,344,000 tax *consumers* supported by 4,568,000 private taxpayers.

For how much longer can the country support this huge Government waste and extravagance, and for how much longer will the *genuine* workers go on working when the fruits of their labors are stolen from them?

JOSEPH FIRTH,
Fairy Meadow, NSW.

Fig 60
(Courtesy of The Melbourne Age)

INCOME TAX FILING

When it comes to that time of year to file income tax returns, July 1, the Australian system is quite a bit simpler than that of the U.S. There are less forms to fill out because the average Australian has much fewer deductions than the average American. Australian deductions are as scarce as hen's teeth. For instance, home mortgage interest is not tax deductible, neither is sales tax, IRA's or consumer interest to mention a few.

In summary, a direct comparison shows that an Australian family of four, earning from $35,000 – $50,000 per year, pays 100% – 150% more in all taxes combined, than does an American family of four in the same income brackets. (See Figure 60)

Please note: Both the U.S. and Australia have announced reductions to their income tax rate for 1987. Some media attention has been given in both countries as to whether these reductions will actually go into effect. If they go into effect the U.S. will make even greater reductions in comparison to the Australian taxation system.

Chapter
Ten

Schools
in
Australia

AN OVERVIEW

Schools in Australia are government owned or privately owned. Each State has a Department of Education that controls the public elementary and high schools within its boarders. The cities do not have any control over the schools.

The private schools within each state are usually run by established churches, such as the Presbyterian, Methodist, Baptist, Catholic and Church of England. A recent survey indicated that private school enrollments may account for up to 50% of all K-12 classes. Most church schools are very well established and receive goodly amounts of government money to keep them running. The federal government actually spends as much or more per student in the private school sector than it does for public school students.

This apparently blatant unconstitutional government support of churches has been unsuccessfully challenged in the courts. Needless to say the courts of Australia are full of ex-private school graduates, as are the federal and state parliaments. (See Figure 61)

Parents still have to pay thousands per year to send their children to private school, so the system succeeds as a method of keeping the educational advantages for those who can pay. Why this persists I will never know. The only hope is that when independence from the British Commonwealth takes place, this sort of assistance to religions will be outlawed by the new constitution. I won't hold my breath though.

Universities and colleges are federally funded and state and federally operated. There are far fewer places at the tertiary education level than the number of people who want to study there. This shortage has something to do with the Australian de-emphasis on higher education. Only 16% of the 18–25 age group is undertaking some form of tertiary education. The U.S. has 54% of the same age group involved in tertiary education. Australia ranks with nations like Turkey, which is definitely not an industrializes state like Australia or the U.S.

When high school seniors sit their finals in Australia, they are competing at the same time in a statewide college entrance examination, scored on a standard curve. Private high school graduates have a long standing tradition of claiming more than their fair-share of college and university places at these state wide exams.

GETTING PAID TO GO TO COLLEGE

The federal government has a program to aid students in college. Colleges and universities have no tuition fees but will introduce an administrative fee of $250 at the beginning of the 1987 school year, and charge only nominal amounts for membership and the use of the student union facilities.

When tuition was abolished and the tax payers started to pay the entire education bill, the Tertiary Education Assistance Scheme was established. This meant that any independent student who qualified for entry into college could receive approximately $60 per week in pay for attending college or university. To qualify for payment, the student had to have lived away from home for two years, or earned a full-time wage for two of the last five years.

What effect does free schooling and paychecks for learning have on the student population? It breeds an attitude of 'we may as well go to college if there is nothing better to do'. Also the cost of failure or dropping out is negligible. They can always go straight on unemployment benefits if they fail at college.

I strongly believe that paying for an education, as is the practice in four year public and private colleges in the U.S., where plentiful funds are available in the form of loans, is the best way to instill the value of an education and its lifelong benefit to the recipient.

Trade schools for the continuing education of apprentices are very common in Australia and take the place of two year junior colleges. Australia still suffers from the crippling British belief that apprenticeship is the proper way to enter the work force as a tradesman. Leave school at 15 or 16 without graduating, spend four years in a training program and the youth will have a trade that will enable him to work for someone else. He will not receive enough education to move successfully to the next level in a career, and not enough education in most cases to start a successful business of his own. Sounds like a great way to keep the workers in their place to me. At least in a two year junior college in the U.S., many subjects studied in connection with a trade can be applied to course credits at a four year college at a later time.

WHAT TYPE OF EDUCATION DO AUSTRALIANS GET?

Elementary schools and high schools are very academic when compared to U.S. public schools. The same is true for colleges and universities. There is by no means the range of social activities in Australian schools that help the students grow as they learn as there are in the U.S. As cities do not control schools, there is not that great sense of community that surrounds American schools and their student body, as can be seen at school football games and town parades across the U.S.

DO AUSTRALIAN SCHOOLS WORK?

By world standards Australia has a very high literacy rate. But the country is not exactly an emerging world industrial and technological giant.

Australia is hemorrhaging at the effects of computers on its society. Australia's backwater mentality of how to run an industrialized nation will make it very difficult for Australia to enter the information age revolution. Australia considers itself an agricultural and mineral resource based economy for the foreseeable future, a fact that will retard its development for decades to come. Australia has a long way to catch up before it can claim to be educating its general population well enough to handle a modern technological society, ready and able to exploit all the opportunities that it creates or that pass its way.

Fig 61

Chapter
Eleven

Housing

AN OVERVIEW

Like the American dream, the Australian dream traditionally includes a single family home in the suburbs. Australians are highly urbanized with 62.75% of the population living in the capital cities, and another 20% or so living in regional urban centers. Regardless of location, single family home ownership is the norm for the average Australian.

The increasing popularity of units, townhouses and condominiums is most probably due to the increased cost of housing in the past 10 to 15 years. However, non-single family home living is usually a second choice for most Australians who buy a place.

The cost of housing in Australia depends as in America, on the location. The closer to downtown the more one pays. The more exclusive and civilized the suburb, the higher the price.

Slums exist in Australia even though most Australians will deny it. True, there may not be the extent of slums as can be found in many American cities, but they do exist. They are more likely than not to come in the form of high rise public housing projects that were built on the sites of tenement housing projects and the living conditions of many Aborigines in remote locations is outright disgusting. But as these conditions are hidden from the general public there is a widely held belief that Australia is a slum-free society.

THE GOVERNMENT AND HOUSING

Unlike the U.S., where the federal government has programs that assist the private housing industry, such as the Federal Housing Authority, the Australian state governments for many years actually built housing in competition with the private construction industry. This construction filled a need for low cost rental housing, and many of these units have been sold to their occupants under extremely favorable long-term mortgages with very low interest rates. This may have been a good program in concept, but it ultimately proved too costly for the government of Victoria. Victoria's state government now purchases already-existing houses and then resells them to lower income families under the same favorable terms. What an average American considers an income to get by on would put him well over the qualifying income to buy one of these subsidized houses. (See Figures 62 & 63)

CONSTRUCTION METHODS

The average suburban Australian house is constructed of hardwood frames, eucalyptus, with a brick veneer exterior. The abundance of clay and other quarry materials for brick manufacture, in addition to lack of native softwoods, dictated this most common form of construction. Double brick (solid brick) housing is an older style of construction honored for its durability. Generally, houses constructed with wood exterior are considered of less value than houses with a brick veneer. Roofs are usually covered with ceramic or concrete tile. Corrugated galvanized iron roofing is used on low-budget non-urban housing all over Australia. Slab and conventional foundations are popular. Slab foundations are being increasingly used throughout Australia.

Lot sizes are generally from 1/4 to 1/5 of an acre; the smaller lot size is more common in the newer subdivisions.

BUYING A HOME IN AUSTRALIA

Existing houses are advertised and sold by offer or sold at public auction by bid. Public auctions for

Govt puts 10-year plans for housing

ADELAIDE: The Labor Party's new housing-construction platform was aimed at achieving greater long-term stability in the industry, the Federal Housing and Construction Minister, Mr Hurford, said in Adelaide yesterday.

Fig 62
(Courtesy of The Melbourne Age)

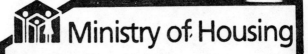 **Ministry of Housing**

URGENTLY NEEDED-STOCK HOMES
EXISTING OR TO-BE-BUILT.

The Ministry of Housing requires additional rental housing stock to meet its needs in the locations nominated.

Offers are invited for completed stock homes or stock homes to be built on builders own land.

The Ministry expects that this housing will provide moderately sized and priced accommodation, representative of a good standard of stock home, conceived and designed to the usual industry criteria and which could be regarded in all respects as a commercially viable project in the private real estate market. The Ministry expects to buy at prevailing market prices with value for money as a principal criterion.

A valuation of the offers will be obtained from the Valuer-General's Office before formal acceptance of any offer.

PREFERRED LOCATIONS & INDICATIVE TOTAL COSTS

Offers should be submitted for areas listed below and total costs, provided by the Valuer-General's Office, are indicated for typical three-bedroom detached villas (100m·-110m·) as upper limits:

LOCATION	CEILING RANGE (JULY 1984) ($)	LOCATION	CEILING RANGE (JULY 1984) ($)
Westernport Region		**Outer Eastern Region**	
Chelsea	60,000-70,000	Croydon	60,000-70,000
Dandenong	57,500-65,000	Ringwood	62,500-72,500
Springvale	62,500-70,000	Knox	62,500-67,500
Frankston	55,500-65,000	Lilydale	60,000-65,000
Mornington	55,000-65,000	Nunawading	65,000-72,500
Southern Region		Sherbrooke	57,500-62,500
Mordialloc	67,000-72,000	Healesville	52,500-57,500
Moorabbin	70,000-75,000	Upper Yarra	52,500-57,500
Oakleigh	70,000-75,000	**Inner Eastern Region**	
Western Region		* Waverley	
Altona	62,500-70,000	* Doncaster	
Sunshine	55,000-67,500	**North-Western Region**	
* Essendon		* Brunswick	
Footscray	60,000-67,500	* Coburg	
		North-Eastern Region	
		Heidelberg	
		Northcote	
		Preston	65,000-75,000

*NOTE: MAXIMUM PURCHASE PRICE LIMIT PER UNIT IS CURRENTLY $75,000

Fig 63
(Courtesy of The Melbourne Age)

houses are very popular in all areas of Australia. New homes are sold quite differently than here in the U.S. One must go to a model or 'display home' as they are referred to in Australia. Here the perspective buyer will see an example of a home that can be built on 'your' land. That's right, the home shopper is looking at a home without land attached in the vast majority of cases. Unlike here in the U.S. where the home shopper selects the model then chooses the lot within the subdivision for an all inclusive price.

The display house in Australia will be most likely a 'base model' with little or no amenities commonly included in the average American new home. Generally all of the following items are extra: carpeting, garage, heating and airconditioning systems, light fittings, fences, plumbing connections, insulation of anything but the roof and ceiling to name but a few. Take a look at similar houses in comparable areas of Australia and the U.S. and compare the features and price. The difference speaks for itself.

PRICE AND FEATURE COMPARISON

Considering that the average lot in Melbourne suburbia is from $35,000 – $40,000, the average housing cost is considerably higher than in the average U.S. If a conservative price of $65,000 is added for land and equivalent amenities to bring the Melbourne house up to the Sacramento standard, the cost would be about $115,000! (See Figure 64)

This is just the exposed cost of a house that is being compared, one has to look at other items such as mortgages to see the real cost of a house in Australia compared to one in the U.S.

MORTGAGES - A HAZARD TO THE CONSUMERS FINANCIAL HEALTH

WARNING: Australian mortgage interest payments are NOT TAX DEDUCTIBLE!!   Severe damage to one's long-term life style can result in paying for an Australian mortgage.

If one buys a house in Australia tomorrow, not one penny of the interest is tax deductible. One eats the interest payments so to speak. So why buy one may ask?   It is just the need to be a homeowner that drives Australians to buying homes.   Also the old advice of buying a home because it will always appreciate in price is often heard.

In Australia the buyer needs 10% to 30% down, must pay 15%-15.5% interest (Dec. 1986) and receives NO INTEREST DEDUCTION! Australian home buyers pay 32%+ more for housing than do people in the U.S. when all the facets of house purchases are considered. Mortgages are secured at banks, with 30% down payment, or Building Societies (Savings and Loans) with as little as 10% down. Closing costs can run to $2,000 because of the charges of lawyers (solicitors as they are locally known) involved in title searches. Do-it-yourself title searches have recently become available by law so this can save the buyer some money. Points are not payable per se, but there are hefty fees included in the closing costs for mortgage origination.

As mentioned earlier, interest and closing costs are not tax deductible when buying a house.   Interest rates are set by the government and compared to U.S. interest rates that can fluctuate wildly, Australian interest rates move much more gradually. Unfortunately for Australians, these gradual interest

HOUSING FEATURE & PRICE COMPARISON

Sacramento & Melbourne (1984)

THE SACRAMENTO HOUSE :
4 bedrooms, 2.5 bathrooms,
Family, Dining, Lounge &
Laundry Rooms. Exterior
Stucco, Slab Foundation,
Two Storey plus Garage.

THE MELBOURNE HOUSE:
4 bedrooms, 2 bathrooms,
Family, Dining, Lounge &
Laundry Rooms. Exterior
Brick Veneer, Slab Found-
ation, 2 Storey.

PRICE: $86,000

$50,000

FEATURES INCLUDED IN PRICE:

Land	Yes	No
Garage	Yes	No
Heating	Yes	No
Aircon.	Yes	No
Water	Yes	No
Elect.	Yes	No
Gas	Yes	No
B. Fence	Yes	No
F. Garden	Yes	No
Insulation	Yes	No
(roof & walls)		
D/Glazing	Yes	No
Carpets	Yes	No
Drapes	Yes	No
Lite Fit.	Yes	No
Dishwsh.	Yes	No
Teleph.	Yes	No
Path/Dwy	Yes	No

* If all features were added to the Melbourne house, the price would rise to approximately $115,000. Since 1984 the inflation rate in Melbourne has been significantly higher than that in Sacramento and housing prices reflect these changes.

Fig 64

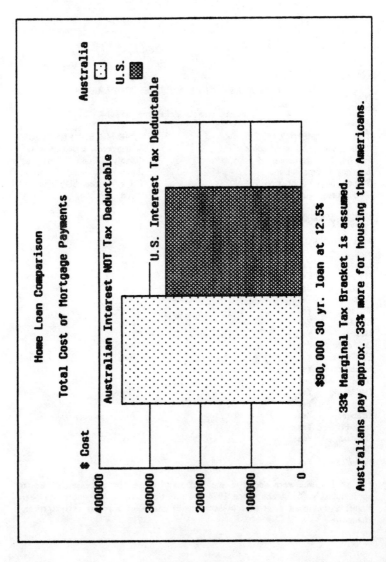

Fig 65

rate moves are only in one direction, up! (See Figure 65)

GOVERNMENT GRANT TO FIRST-TIME HOME BUYERS

The Victorian government grants up to $7000 over a five year period to help with the purchase or down payment for the first-time home buyer. This appears to be attractive, but the Catch 22 of the matter is that one has to have a low income to qualify for the grant. As an example this allows my unmarried brother with a moderate income to qualify for the grant, whereas good friends of ours with two incomes have trouble saving for a down payment but earn too much to qualify for the grant. A great help to the middle income people indeed.

WHERE MOST PEOPLE LIVE

Generally the larger the city or town the higher the cost of housing. In descending order of cost, the housing reduces in price as follows: Sydney, Melbourne, Brisbane, Adelaide, Canberra, Perth, Hobart and Darwin. Variations occur in different parts of each urban area, of course, but this is a general guide only.

SYDNEY, pronounced 'Sinee', the capital of New South Wales, is Australia's metropolis. Big, 3,310,500 people in the city and suburbs, Sydney is built around one of the most attractive harbors in the world. The weather is sub-tropical. That means indoor plants grow outdoors like weeds; it has plenty of rain; it is humid in summer and not very cold in winter. Sydney's smog rivals that of Los Angeles and Tokyo and is a constant cause for concern. Sydney is the business and cultural center of Australia and a favorite stop for foreign tourists. Even some

Melbournians will admit to liking Sydney because it is more exciting than Melbourne.

MELBOURNE, the capital of Victoria and pronounced 'Melbin', is the banking and financial center of Australia. Built on a plain like Los Angeles, it faces a very large protected harbor. The weather can best be described as Mediterranean. Humid in the summer with afternoon thunderstorms; overcast, wet winters with cold winds and some fog. It actually rains in Melbourne 50% of the year. The Garden State, as Victoria is known, is no more evident than in Melbourne and its suburbs. Private and public gardens cover the city.

Melbourne's smog rivals that of Los Angeles many times each year and is also of continuing concern to the people of Melbourne. In fact, recently published reports on smog list Tokyo, Los Angeles, Sydney and Melbourne all competing as cities with the most heavily polluted air in the world. Australia has just recently introduced unleaded fuel and this may eventually help the situation.

BRISBANE, capital of Queensland and pronounced 'Brizbun', is in the tropical north east, an area also referred to as 'The Deep North' by Australian southerners. Brisbane has a similar climate to Hawaii, if you like that sticky feeling for half the year, and is a much smaller city than either Sydney or Melbourne. Queensland plays the same role as Florida as the "retirement state for Australia's oldsters". Queensland is also commonly referred to as 'The Banana Republic' because of its super conservative and outspoken Premier, Joh Bejelke-Petersen. (See Figure 66)

ADELAIDE, the capital of South Australia, is indeed a nice city. Located on the south coast further north than Melbourne, and enjoying a milder climate because of it, Adelaide is a small but culturally active city. Nearby is the famous Barossa Valley wine country, producing some of the world's finest table wines.

PERTH, the capital of Western Australia, has been aptly described as a pretty San Diego. It has a fine west–coast climate but is 2,000 miles from the more densely populated regions of Australia. Having my father's side of the family from the west, it sometimes seemed like Perth is 2000 days behind the rest of Australia and its thinking. Western Australians often find it easier and less expensive to vacation in Hong Kong than visit the east coast of their own country.

CANBERRA, pronounced 'CanBra', the capital of Australia, located in the Australian Capital Territory, is a small–scale Washington D.C.. Full of public servants with unrealistic housing prices and a bureaucratic cleanliness about the place, it is cold in winter with occasional snow and hot in the summer.

HOBART, the capital of Tasmania – that small land mass off the southern tip of the mainland – is a small city of 172,000 people. Cold in winter with snow on occasions, some wild rivers and rugged bush lands it is a great place to vacation and to view the relics of some of the very first settlements in Australia.

DARWIN, the capital of the Northern Territory, is in the extreme far north of tropical Australia. A multicultural city, it is typical of tropical living complete with all the dangers of cyclones (hurricanes), one of which happened to level the entire city Christmas eve of 1973. Like Perth, Darwin is 2000 miles from the more metropolitan East and is probably proud of the fact.

Fig 66

Chapter
Twelve

Crime
and
Punishment
in
Australia

AN OVERVIEW

Americans have an enormous inferiority complex about the amount of crime in the U.S. There is a perception in this country that crime is at an all time high, and that no household or family can survive without the fear of being crime victims at some time.

In fact, the overall crime rates in the U.S. have fallen in recent years and they continue to do so. According to the Federal Bureau of Investigation, the average reduction in the eight major crime areas that include Murder, Rape, Robbery, Aggravated Assault, Burglary, Larceny-theft and Motor Vehicle theft was an overall 6.57% from 1982 to 1983. While Australia does not keep and publish national crime statistics (maybe they don't feel they are important or it is a convenient way for the population at large to be kept in the dark about the real extent of crime in Australia) Victoria's crime rate, which can be considered a fair guide to the nation as a whole, in these groups increased 2.06% between 1982 and 1983.

The U.S. is dealing with its crime problem in some substantial manner, and there appears to be no let up in this recent resolve to abate crime in its many forms. In contrast, Australians as a whole have this self proclaimed belief that they live in a low crime society, especially when compared to the U.S. While the crime rates are clearly lower in Australia, approximately 65%-70% of U.S. levels on a crimes per 100,000 population basis, violent crime is currently increasing at an astounding rate and is even higher than the U.S. based on population size.

GUN CONTROL

The Australian general public has always been subjected to the propaganda ploy of blaming American crime rates on the availability of handguns. While this seems somewhat logical at first glance, the absurdity is evident when the facts are known.

The supporters of handgun bans, among other arguments, use the old tactic of "If handguns are outlawed, then the criminals would have a greatly reduced selection of concealable weapons to use for crimes", and this in some way would reduce their ability to commit crimes. In Australia, where handguns are virtually out of reach for the average citizen, crimes are not abandoned because of lack of handguns. To obtain a handgun in most Australian states, one can join a pistol club for $100's per year. After six months membership using the club's handguns, the club member can apply to the state for a handgun permit for sporting purposes only. If the member's record is clean and there is no problem with the paperwork, nine months after joining he can buy a handgun. An individual in the security business can own a handgun. But, if one stops working in that industry, or lets the permit expire, there will be a knock at the door one night and two big state policemen will ask for the weapon. It will not be returned unless the permit is re-established through work or a pistol club.

This appears to be a good, safe and controlled situation, an analysis that is reasonable to expect from a civilized country. The only problem is, the criminal in Australia can get a handgun anytime he desires and there is nothing anyone can do about it. All criminals have their sources for weapons, and handguns are on that list. Beyond this though is another area of myth. Rifles and shotguns are readily available to the general public of Australia, and consequently these items are used for armed holdups and other crimes. They are modified and concealed to play the role the handgun does in many American crime situations. I do not support the

National Rifle Association or any similar organization now or in the past, but its slogan to fight gun control, "Outlaw guns, and only the outlaws will have guns", is so true in the Australian experience.

A greater moral and ethical issue at the heart of Australian gun control laws is the fact that Australia is still in many ways a British colony, so to speak. America's history shows that the British were ejected from U.S. soil by guns; the use of rifles by the colonist patriot, who used them to break away from tyranny. After the U.S. experience, the British made certain that they would not make the same mistake in another colony. Australia was settled and developed with few arms being held by the civilian population. While at times this worked well for the sake of law and order, it simply translated into the fact that the Australian government could declare marshall law at any time with only little danger of armed resistance from the general public. In the U.S. there would be battles, doorstep-to-doorstep, in a fruitless attempt to get the population under control.

The reason for most gun ownership in the U.S., I thought, was for household protection from random criminal acts that law enforcement agencies could not prevent. But there is a deeper and more profound reason for the vast amount of weapons in private hands in the U.S. After distilling gun owner's feelings and thoughts for four years, I have concluded that gun ownership is a form of insurance to ensure a democratic way of life in the U.S. Unlike the Australian people's attitude toward their own government, the government of the United States is considered a potential enemy of the people, and if the constitutional system of checks and balances fails and a totalitarian state emerges (I do not consider this at all probable) then the people of America could again take up the call to armed intervention and re-establish the Republic.

From a social point of view, the American people are a far more law abiding people than just about any other nation on earth. Why make such a pretentious claim? Simply put, with more guns than population, the vast majority of Americans must be very law abiding because this country would be in complete chaos if people decided to use their weapons for other than defensive purposes.

THE POLICE

I worked as a Railway Inspector, a fancy name for an unarmed police officer, on the Victorian Railways for some time and got to see the 'real' city life of Melbourne. It also made me very aware of how inadequate and dangerous the legal/justice system of Australia is.

To start with, the State provides the law enforcement agencies for the general population. The local police are State Police and they handle anything from crime to major traffic and highway patrol duties. Minor city traffic violations and regulations are handled by City By-Laws/Traffic enforcement officers. (I was one of those for a while also.) Australia, or more specifically Victoria, has a police ratio of one officer for every 6000 persons. A disastrous situation when you consider that the average law enforcement density in the U.S. in 1982 was two officers per 1,000 population. Australia has only 1/12 the number of public safety officers as the U.S. per 1,000 population but has a crime rate two thirds the level of the U.S..

It was not something I thought much about until I visited Australia after having lived almost four years in the United States. Frankly, I felt somewhat unnerved by the fact that there were so few police officers around. This situation easily explains the slow response time of the Australian police to calls for assistance compared to their U.S. counterparts. In our calls for police assistance on even the most minor matters here in California, the response has been fast and efficient every time. I know that it doesn't work that way all the time for everyone, but it is comforting to know how close help is.

Another serious problem with some Australian state police departments is the fact that it is not a police standing order that all officers be armed while on duty. A police officer in Victoria can choose not to be armed on duty. Think about how you would feel if you called the police in a life threatening situation and the officer arrives without a weapon? Great, just the sort of thing you need, right! Some lunatic has a gun pointed at you, or has committed some heinous crime, and the police officer is going to talk him into stopping and giving up? Sure! The states also have wildlife officers and rangers to patrol the bush (forest) and to protect the natural heritage of Australia. Australia's unique flora and fauna, combined with strict export laws, is a great source of contraband for animal and bird smugglers.

The federal government has its usual array of law enforcement departments including the Federal Police, the equivalent of the Federal Bureau of Investigation; Australian Security Intelligence Organization, the counterpart of the CIA, and the Customs Officers at the airports and docks to control people and contraband.

THE COURTS

The lowest level court in Australia is the Justice of the Peace attached to the Magistrate's Court.

The JP's court handles minor citations and infractions of the law. In Victoria a panel of three JP's hears the case and then confers to hand down the decision. No major offenses are ever heard here.

The next higher level of court is the Magistrate's Court. More serious offenses are heard at this level, those involving misdemeanors and initial hearings for felonies. The defendant has the right at this stage in misdemeanor hearings to opt for trial without jury if he/she so desires.

At each stage so far the defendant has access to legal council, but it is not provided as a rule if one does not ask for it or cannot pay for it. If the defendant needs legal assistance he pays for it, or goes unrepresented.

Also, Australians are less advanced when it comes to dealing with the legal system than their U.S. brothers. Australians are less likely to defend their own rights in situations of apparent minor consequence. There is almost a sense of passive indifference to the legal system that results in the desire to get the hassle of the court proceedings out of the way as quickly as possible.

The most glaring deficiency of the entire Australian judicial system is at the magistrates court level, where, at worst, one can be jailed for a conviction. There is no public prosecutor's office or district attorney's office in these lower level cases to screen the prosecution briefs to make sure that they are prepared properly by the enforcement agency. Prosecutors are usually senior officers of the law enforcement agency that filed the prosecution brief. Because of this situation there is considerable collusion between the enforcement officers and the prosecutors in the arena of the Magistrate's Court. The natural consequence of such collusion is a tendency to 'cook' evidence and reports made by the officers to suit the purposes of the prosecution.

While employed in the Victorian Railways Investigation Division, I was asked a number of times to perjure myself on behalf of other officers just to 'brick' some punk who had given the arresting officers a particularly bad time during booking or investigation. I never complied with such requests, and at the same time I made it well known that I was not the officer to seek out for perjured statements for the withholding of information during internal departmental investigations. Because of my stand it was amazing how many of my fellow officers requested not to work with me.

The County Court is the court for jury tried felonies, except murder, and for persons accused of misdemeanors who request a trial by jury.

The archaic traditions of the British legal system permeate this level of the justice system. Defendants in the magistrates court may be represented by counsel, a solicitor (attorney), who does not have to be a member of the 'Bar'. Defendants in the County Court or higher court, must be represented by a solicitor, but if the solicitor is not a member of the 'Bar' also, the solicitor must engage counsel for this higher court in the form of a Barrister, and as their name may suggest, are licensed to practice at the 'Bar'. Thus the defendant has to pay two legal fees to be represented in serious cases. Solicitors do the hack work of the legal profession as do attorneys in the U.S.

The first court of appeal in the state of Victoria is the Victorian Supreme Court. It is also the court for murder trials.

The Victorian Court of Appeal is the final court for all state law matters.

The Australian High Court is the final court of appeal and also determines constitutional law.

The key to all Australian courts is that they are not recognized as a separate branch of the Australian power base. The courts are totally at the mercy of the administration and the legislators in regard to any decisions the courts make. It is quite common to expect the law to be changed by act of parliament if the legislature doesn't like it or it conflicts with friends of their party.

In review then, if one is fast enough that the lack of police can't catch him, or powerful enough to have friends in parliament who will change the law for him, or maybe one is just rich enough to pay for plenty of defense attorneys, then one could probably do a good job at being a criminal in Australia. By the way, they don't execute anyone in Australia any more because they think it is barbaric.

WHAT IT MEANS TO THE AVERAGE AUSTRALIAN

The way the legal justice system actually operates and affects the average person is very different from that in the U.S.

In Australia, a driver can be pulled over in his vehicle in any state without probable cause. Anytime a police officer, properly identified, asks a motorist to pull over and stop the vehicle, the driver must comply or he is breaking the law. After stopping the auto, the officer has the right to inspect the driver's license and I.D., to check the registration and to search the car for anything. Evidence found during this random search that leads to a criminal prosecution is 100% admissible in court.

To be pulled over your vehicle does not have to fit the description of a stolen vehicle; the driver does not have to fit the description of a suspect in a crime; nor does the driver have to be showing signs of erratic driving. I know that this system can never be instituted in the U.S. because of concerns for privacy violations and the need for probable cause in these circumstances. However, knowing a number of Australian police officers, this perfectly legal Australian tactic of randomly stopping vehicles, is used to check out those undesirable elements the police officers may come across while on patrol. For example, random vehicle stops are used extensively against bikers , hot rodders, junky car drivers and other non-conformists in the eyes of the police. As outrageous as this system sounds in the context of U.S. law, random vehicle stops are an amazingly effective anti-crime tool, uncovering a vast amount of crime before during or after the fact. It has been reported these stops uncover something more than 50% of all criminal acts prosecuted in Victoria.

When an Australian is arrested, he is by law supposed to be read his rights in form of a warning. There is no guarantee that the warning will be given before he his hauled off to the station for booking and questioning. The arrested individual has no guaranteed right anywhere during this procedure to call an attorney or to make one phone call. He has no guaranteed right to have someone present while he is initially questioned, although he may get a lawyer if the police don't want to proceed with the booking regardless.

Australians have a basic mistrust of police, probably stemming from the harsh days of British tyranny during the colonial period. On the other hand, I feel that the majority of Americans feel sympathetic towards the American police and will support them whenever possible. The neighborhood watch program is a very clear indication of this support for local policing agencies. Australia, is just now developing the neighborhood watch program.

A small indication of the increase in the Australian crime rate is the number of our friends and acquaintances who had their homes burglarized in the three plus years we had been away from Australia prior to our last visit. Before leaving Australia, I can honestly say I had very little contact with crime victims. When we returned it seemed that every fourth person had been touched by burglary in the recent past.

The reader should by now be aware that the law works very differently in Australia, and one's position as a citizen or resident, held in the highest regard in the U.S., is not protected from the government, police or other citizens in Australia by a bill of rights. The day that Australia gets a bill of rights will be the day that it turns into a fully democratic republic, established on the basis of the highest regard for the freedom and rights of the individuals in Australia. (See Figure 67)

Prostitution in parlors to be legal

Prostitution will be legal in massage parlors which have planning permits, under reforms announced by the Victorian Government yesterday.

Fig 67
(Courtesy of The Melbourne Age)

Chapter
Thirteen

Sports,
Recreation
and
Entertainment

TANDBERG

THE LAND OF THE LONG WEEK-END

Australians love their public holidays, so much so, that they, with tongue in cheek, refer to their country as the 'Land of the Long Week-End'. Many Australian holidays fall on Fridays, and like their American counterparts, Australians are apt to head out of town at every opportunity.

One interesting difference with the Australian obsession with holidays and vacations, is that they have over a period of time become masters at being able to think up the most feeble excuses for extra holidays. The effects of these holidays on the country is exacerbated even more by the fact that so many people work for the government. Just as in the U.S., government workers in Australia tend to get more paid holidays than those employed by private enterprise.

Let us begin at the beginning.

NEW YEAR'S DAY is a well established holiday in Australia. So well established and enthused with the holiday spirit at large, most Australians have the day after New Years as a holiday as well.

AUSTRALIA DAY occurs on January 26th. This holiday is sort of like America's Independence Day July the 4th, except that Australia only pretends to be independent from Great Britain. The holiday is moved around to accommodate a Monday or Friday of course. No overflow again, only one day is taken.

February and March are very lean months, with no time out for the average worker except Labor Day, yet another long week-end.

April and Easter, or late March if that is the case, sees an unusual swag (that's Australian for a bed roll or bag that an itinerant carries his belongings in, it means 'alot') of holidays that mystifies most every other 'Christian' nation. Australians are no more church going, or God fearing people than the average American, rather less so if anything. Never ones to miss a great opportunity to 'Avagoodweekend', many Australians unashamedly have five days off including the week-end at Easter.

First there is GOOD FRIDAY, which all people get, Christian or not,then there is the week-end with Easter Sunday.

Then comes EASTER MONDAY, a pure invention of the Australian imagination for another religious holiday, and last but not least comes EASTER TUESDAY. Many get this extra day in the Australian Imaginary Religious Calendar.

ANZAC DAY (Australia and New Zealand Army Corps) in April, is much like Veterans Day in the U.S. This holiday fall uncharacteristically on a Thursday. Most Australians make an effort to get around this minor inconvenience by scheduling a vacation day for the Friday after to make a four day week-end.

May offers no fix to the 'Long-week-end-a-holics' to get them through till June.

All Australian republican and independence overtures not withstanding, never let it be said that Australians let their heart-felt beliefs get in the way of another holiday. June harbors the enigma of colonial dominance, thrust in Australia's face each year, THE QUEEN'S BIRTHDAY!

July, August, September and October are void of public holidays, except for Melbourne which hosts The Royal Melbourne Show (Victorian State Fair). The entire Melbourne metropolitan area has a one day holiday for the state fair that runs for two weeks. If one has ever gone to The Show on SHOW DAY, it seems like everyone in Melbourne is there on that day anyway.

November has one of the most questionable holidays in the world. Many people in the Melbourne metropolitan area take a declared holiday that arises on the first Tuesday of the month. Would it be election day? No way, Australians do their voting on Saturdays. This sacred day, called CUP DAY, is dedicated to The Melbourne Cup. A most famous horse race, like the Kentucky Derby, that has been run for nearly 100 years. One thing is for sure though, nearly every T.V. and radio in the nation are tuned to that race just after 2pm on the first Tuesday of November.

December offers the usual CHRISTMAS DAY vacation plus the day after Christmas, called BOXING DAY. No, Australians don't watch the fights on T.V. the day after Christmas. This is an archaic holiday invented in England. The legend goes that the people used to 'box' food and clothing for the poor on this day after Christmas for charity. It is now more likely that one will find Australians 'boxing' six packs of beer for their own consumption during this summer festive day.

Do all these holidays take your breath away? Compared to my six days here in the U.S., the 13 I would still get if living in Melbourne seem like a worker's prayer answered. But look at this in terms of the nation's productivity. In Australia there are only 247 work days per year, the shortest among western nations and only a few more than the Roman Empire before it collapsed. Those additional up to seven days per year cost Australia 2.7% of its productivity. An amount even a healthy economy can ill afford to lose.

SPORTS AND SPORTSMANIA

The national summer sport in Australia, in schools, colleges, by amateurs and professionals alike, is 'cricket'. Most of you who are old movie buffs will have seen those English films where players dressed all in white play a rather slow game with strange bats and weird pitches. This snail's pace game, that can last up to five days in international professional competition, is a pure import from Britain.

But when the skies turn to winter in Australia, the 'real' sports are played across the nation. Depending on what state one resides in, the winter sport may be Rugby or Australian Rules Football.

Rugby is the British game that shares some similarities with American football and is played as an international sport among many of the British Commonwealth and ex-Commonwealth countries. Australian players generally consider themselves to be better, that is to say more rugged sportsmen than their American football counterparts. To demonstrate their ruggedness they don't wear any padding or helmet, unlike those 'pansy yanks'. Needless to say there are no university or college qualifications required to play rugby professionally.

Australian Rules Football is familiar to many Americans because of the cable T.V. sports channel ESPN, which has been broadcasting 'The Match of the Day' from Melbourne, Victoria for the past couple of years. For the uninitiated, this game of 'aerial ping-pong' as it is sometimes referred to, is a combination of soccer, rugby, basketball and volleyball. It is played with a ball like a rugby ball (American football with rounder ends), and the players are allowed to kick, pass, bounce and dribble the ball around the field, or 'oval' as it is called because of the actual shape of the field.

There is an army of player on the field at any given time, 18 from each team, and six referees, or umpires (umpees) as they are locally known. A game is more of a test of endurance than of skill. With a few breaks a game usually lasts about two and one half hours. These brave souls, who are considered the epitome of Australian sportsmen, like rugby players wear no padding to speak of and snicker at their American pro football counterparts that have to lug around almost 30 pounds of protective, but sensible gear.

If one is of British or European extraction, soccer will be the favorite fare for winter sports. Loving dubbed 'Wog Ball' by some ocker (red neck) wit, because of the wide participation by immigrants, this is not really a national sport held in the same regard as rugby and Australian Rules. No 'real' Australian male would be caught dead watching soccer on a Saturday afternoon if there was a good football (footy) game on the box.

Amateur sports participation is wide spread and Australia proudly claims to be a land of sportsmen and sportswomen. Alas this is not quite the case. Like Americans, the average Australian watches much more sport on T.V. than he or she actually participates in. The most exercise the average Australian sports fanatic gets is the walk to the T.V. to change channels, and to lift the 12oz can while imbibing some of that famed Australian brew.

A country of only 16 million people would appear not to be able to support much in the way of professional sports teams. Wrong! Australia is so sports mad, ever more so than the U.S., that the amount of sports hype is overwhelming, especially for those of us who do not care to see grown men mutilate each other on the field of battle in the name of good sportsmanship and popular entertainment.

Melbourne, Victoria, my home town with a population of about three million , supports no less than 12 professional football teams. Add the 18 semi-professional football teams (the minor leagues) and the senses are numbed at the thought of this insanity.

Do these teams make money? They do. With six games each week during the season, each game attracts crowds as large as 30,000 –50,000 fans. Add television advertising revenues and merchandising royalties to the gate receipts and the football industry is very lucrative.

The atmosphere at these football games can be exhilarating, especially because fans can bring in an unlimited amount of alcoholic beverages in their own containers. With this kind of relaxed atmosphere it gives every fan a 'fair go' at utilizing beverage containers to persuade the umpires in their decision making process.

In late 1986 plans were announced to make Australian Rules Football a national game by moving some teams to Sydney from Melbourne, and increase the number of teams in the league. There are some solid financial considerations behind such a move.

SCHOOL SPORTS

Australian school sports programs are nowhere as extensive as those in the U.S. Most sporting competitions in public schools are held during regular school hours. Therefore parents get very little chance to participate in their children's school sporting activities.

Local sports teams though do play on week-ends. Like Little League and Pop Warner football, there are cricket and football teams for Australian children to participate in outside the school environment.

There is no formal path to professional sports through the schools or colleges of Australia. Amateur competition leads to the professional ranks.

MOVIES, TELEVISION, THEATER AND MUSIC

Australian artistic tastes and endeavors are very similar to, albeit not as extensive, and very influenced by their American brothers. A quick glance at any local television guide in Australia will show program origins of roughly 34% Australian, 33% American and 33% British or European. I grew up watching many notable U.S. television shows and have many fond memories for the likes of Bugs Bunny, The Cisco Kid, Superman, Leave It To Beaver, Lassie and others too numerous to mention. Foreign English language shows are so popular in Australia that the government, which owns several T.V. and radio networks, enacted a law to force a certain percentage of programming to be Australian. The government doesn't concern itself with the quality of the domestic programming, just the quantity of it.

Watching the network nightly news in Australia, any American would instantly recognize the theme music and sets as being clones of the U.S. networks. As similar as these are, Australians think that they live in a world that isn't really too much like America.

The Australian movie industry had a few boom years recently, with such films as Mad Max, The Year of Living Dangerously and The Man from Snowy River. 1984 was one of the worst in Australian film history. One reason may be that all the top directors, namely Peter Weir, Bruce Berresford and Fred Scepsci, are now residing in the U.S. and making brilliant films. Things do change though. The movie Crocodile Dundee, staring Paul Hogan, Mr. Come See Australia himself, was so well made and promoted that it became the largest grossing foreign film and the largest grossing fall movie of all time in the U.S. in late 1986. With revenues of US$100 million and still going strong, more Australian producers should take note of what makes for a world beater movie like Dundee.

Australians too often have to go overseas to receive their due reward. Australia looks on talent as something of an anomaly. It's great to have people who are talented, but they are viewed as more or less normal people and are not accorded any great acclaim. There is no 'star system' in Australia like that that exists in the U.S. If one wants to be appreciated to the highest level, and receive compensation in line with ones world class abilities, then one must leave Australia for America or Europe. Unfortunately, the act of leaving Australia for greener pastures in other lands is considered almost treason by the average Australian. There is a consensus of opinion that the talented artist or the professional feels that he or she is now too good to live in the land that gave them their start in life. Australians will not gratify you with great praise and stardom if you excel Australia is fortunate to have a rich pool of talent in the arts. There is no lack of world class performers in all areas. Recent U.S. invasions by Australian rock bands and other musicians is clear evidence of the great talent Australia has been producing for many years, and will continue to do so for the forseeable future. (See Figure 68)

GAMBLING - THE NATIONAL PASTIME

The one national pastime shared by almost all adult Australians is gambling. Not so much in casinos, as there are very few in Australia, but in the form of lotteries, horse races, football games, harness racing and greyhound racing from one end of the country to another. Australians have earned such a reputation for gambling that it is said that Australians would bet on two flies crawling up a wall if there was no other bettable activity to be found. Australians are probably the world's foremost gamblers, spending vast sums of money each year trying their luck with some form of legalized betting.

Every local shopping area has a Totalizator Agency Board (TAB), a small betting shop that is a branch of a semi-government body that controls all the legal off-course track betting in its state. A typical Saturday in Melbourne would allow one to bet on one main metropolitan race meeting, one just out-of-town country meeting, the professional football games in town, numerous interstate horse and harness race meetings in daylight, then an array of local and interstate harness and greyhound races that evening. Each day of the week, except Sunday, the same betting opportunities are available in varying degrees. This whole system is duplicated nation wide.

Lotteries were probably invented in Australia; at least one would think so considering how popular they are. In Melbourne there is a 'lotto' game twice a week, instant tickets daily, regular lottery tickets weekly and some variations to boot. Most all the revenues go to supporting the massive government bureaucracies and hospital programs. With seven major hospitals in a three mile radius of downtown Melbourne, it is no wonder they need all those gambling dollars.

One thing is common to all gambling in Australia. That is the fact that one can participate in almost all forms of gambling with as little as 50 cents or one dollar for one unit. Perhaps this is why gambling is so popular, everyone can participate at his corner store for $4.00 and bet on an eight race card.

Australians clearly live an Americanized lifestyle, modified for local conditions. For the visiting American, there is no end to the places that he or she can observe the average Australian recreating to his heart's content. The major cities of Australia hold gourmet delights of every kind, theater performances of the highest caliber and unique places to see and things to do. Miles of accessible beaches and large tracts of remote forests allow even the most adventurous of natives and visitors alike to be fully occupied most of the time.

SUNDAY

Channel 0
And Channel 28 on UHF

PM
3.15 La Domenica Sportiva
3.15 Paths to Art
4.00 Bamse The Strongest Bear
6.15 The Flute And The Bomba-
dea (R)
6.30 News with Karina Kelly.
7.00 Inside Japan — Final
program in the BBC docu-
mentary series. ★

7.30 Soccer
8.30 The Sunday Show
8.30 Movie: Two Halves Of The
Heart, a 1982 Yugoslav
drama (Serbo-Croatian)
11.10 News (R)
11.40 Close

Our TV stars, as selected by
Anna Murdoch, rate as
follows:
★ Worth considering
★★ Excellent
★★★ Not to be missed

Critic's Choice

In Grand Duo: the final of Stuart
Wagstaff's World Playhouse
(Channel 2, 8.30 pm), a surprising
offer to two middle-aged amateur
pianists causes panic in their families. Excellent drama starring
Prunella Scales, Judy Parfitt, An-
thony Bate, Bernard Horsfall and
Richard Austin.

Channel 2

AM
10.10 Playmates
11.00 Divine Service
PM
12.00 Living Tomorrow
12.15 Sew What (R)
12.30 Countryside (R)
1.00 Four Corners (R)
1.30 Tennis. The final of the
GWA Classic, from the Chan-
dler Sports Centre in Brisbane. Commentators are
Ross Case, Geoff Masters
and Peter Meares.
6.00 Considera
6.55 Weather
7.00 News with Edwin Maher.
7.15 Weekend Magazine

7.40 A Descant For Gossips.
Final program in the ABC
drama serial about a sen-
sitive young girl in a
small community. (S) ★

8.30 Stuart Wagstaff's World
Playhouse. Final pro-
gram in the series. To-
night 'Grand Duo'. A
startling offer to two
middle-aged amateur
pianists causes alarm and
upheaval. (PGR) ★

9.25 News And Weather
9.30 A Matter Of Chance. New
series on the plight of the
disabled. (R)
10.00 World Of Music: Tonight,
Sir Georg Solti conducts the
Chicago Symphony Orches-
tra in Beethoven's Symphony No. 1.
10.60 Close

Channel 7

AM
7.30 It is Written
8.00 Marathon. The running of
the Big M Marathon.
10.00 World Of Sport Replay
11.00 World Of Sport

PM
2.60 Movie: Money From Home,
a 1954 comedy starring
Dean Martin and Jerry Lewis. (R)

4.00 Hogan In London (R)
5.00 Fame (R)
6.00 News, Sport And Weather
with Sandy Roberts.
6.30 The Wonderful World Of
Disney. Summer Magic' (R)
7.30 Willesee 'Family Crisis'.
Willesee examines the worl
of Redbank House, Sydney.
8.30 Movie: California Suite,
a 1978 comedy based on a
play by Neil Simon about
four separate stories that
take place at the Beverly
Hills Hotel, California. It
stars Alan Alda and Jane
Fonda. (AO) ★

10.30 Movie: No Man Of Her
Own, a 1932 mystery about a
gambler who tries to keep
his wife innocent of his activities. It stars Clark Gable
and Carole Lombard. (B&W)
(R)

AM
12.05 Insight (PGR) (R)
12.35 Close

Channel 9

AM
8.00 World Of Survival (R)
5.30 Sound Of Sunday
7.00 Turn Round Australia
7.30 Here's Humphrey
8.30 Point of View
5.30 Religious Feature
9.00 Sunday. Public affairs
program. ★
11.00 Sports Sunday
PM
12.00 Movie: Tail Gunner Joe (R)

2.45 Movie: Horse Feathers,
1932 comedy with The
Marx Brothers. (B&W)
(R) ★

4.00 Land Of The Giants (R)
5.00 The Road Runner (R)
5.30 Candid Camera (R)
6.00 News, Sport And Weather
7.30 New Faces
7.30 60 Minutes

8.30 Movie: The Prisoner Of
Zenda, a 1979 comedy
about a London cab driv-
er who is abducted by the
Duke of Zenda. It stars
Peter Sellers and Elke
Sommer. (PGR) ★

10.30 Taxi
11.00 Golf. The 1983 World Match
Play Championship.

AM
1.35 Movie: Who Is The Black
Dahlia? (PGR) (R)
3.45 Movie: The Captive Heart
(PGR) (B&W) (R)
5.10 Dangerman (PGR) (B&W)
(R)

Channel 10

AM
6.00 The World Tomorrow
6.30 You Say The Word (R)
7.30 An Hour Of Power
8.30 Mass For You At Home
9.00 Let's Go Greek
10.00 Greek Variety Show
11.00 Variety Italian Style

PM
12.00 Movie: Disorderly Orderly,
a 1964 comedy starring Jerry Lewis and Glenda Far-
rell. (R)
1.45 Movie: Robin And The
Seven Hoods, a 1964 musical
comedy starring Frank Sina-
tra and Dean Martin. (R)

4.00 The Six Million Dollar Man
5.00 Solid Gold
6.00 News, Sport And Weather
6.30 John Laws's Week 'The
Earth Beneath Me'.
7.30 M.A.S.H. (PGR)
8.00 Classic M.A.S.H. (PGR) (R)

8.30 Movie: The Exorcist, a
modified for television 1973
horror about a priest who is
called on to exorcise a
12-year-old girl whose body
has been possessed by the
Devil. It stars Linda Blair
and Max von Sydow. (AO)
10.50 Entertainment This Week
11.30 City Lights

AM
1.00 Catch Hollywood In The
Act (R)
1.30 Close

Fig 68
(Courtesy of The Melbourne Age)

Chapter
Fourteen

Ten
Steps
to
Australia's
Future

FULFILLING THE AUSTRALIAN PROMISE

The best way that I can summarize how Australians feel about themselves and their country, but would never admit, is that they are 'closet Americans'.

It is this 'closet' approach, their lackluster approach to life and achievement, their 'she'll be right mate' attitude that dulls inspiration in all facets of Australian life, that retards the emergence of a vitality needed to face the facts of living in the twentieth century in an industrialized western nation.

Australia is strapped predominantly to narrow outlooks on the world that have the greatest negative effect on Australia's future. Although Australia's cultural traditions were imported from Britain and Southern Europe, Australia enjoys much the same lifestyle as most middle class Americans.

Australia has a grandiose view of itself in relation to the rest of the world. It has gone as far as designating itself as 'The Lucky Country' and 'God's Own Country', although New Zealanders would fight for their right to exclusive use of the latter.

An enormous, sparsely populated outpost of British colonialism in South East Asia, Australia is 'The Lucky Country' and 'God's Own Country' to millions of British, Southern European and Vietnamese immigrants. Unfortunately for Australia and her people, this 'old world' frame of reference left over from Britain and Europe has done much to stunt the potential of this bountiful land and its resourceful population.

This jaundiced outlook on the world is painfully evident to any foreign visitor. No matter where the American tourist travels in Australia he will generally find that the Australian people are more than friendly towards Americans. It is a different story however when it comes to the Australian's feeling towards America. One is as likely to hear hostile comments on America and Americanization, as to hear compliments about American culture. Australians can be rather blunt and rude in the matter of discussing someone else's homeland and actually putting it down regardless of present company, because of the conceit they have developed under 'The Lucky Country' frame of reference. On the contrary, while living in the U.S., I have never heard an American in casual conversation make a derogatory remark about Australia. If one dares to criticize Australia in front of the natives they get really annoyed and will let you know it. Australians are quick to criticize and put down the U.S. for its failures and seldom give credit where credit is due for U.S. successes. It is as though Australians hate to admit the 'The American Way' is so far superior in a multitude of respects than 'The Australian Way', when it comes to serving the average man's interests and needs.

An American tourist can be in Australia for two minutes and an Australian will come up to him and ask how he likes the place. Australians as a nation have an enormous inferiority complex and are forever seeking the approval of their western allies in world affairs.

What comes to mind recently was the well publicized (in Australia) chance that Australia might act as the middleman for U.S. and Soviet talks. This proposal is only one of the long line of attempts to bolster the Australians' self image by attempting to 'play with the big kids on the block'.

While not under estimating Australia's role as an important strategic ally of the U.S., as a nation Australia lacks a perspective of its world importance. Often drunk with this self importance, a long running game the 'Socialist Left' of the Australian Labor

Party plays everytime mention is made of U.S. bases in Australia is to demand their immediate removal. The U.S. has some of its largest foreign intelligence gathering bases in Australia as part of the now threatened ANZUS defense treaty.

Australia's basic insecurities, fed by the restricted mass media and its continual withholding of the facts about the real world has led to a nation without a clear destiny.

Australia is a nation that physically escaped its past in Europe, but is incapable of realizing its full potential because of its reluctance to learn from the most appropriate role model on earth, the U.S.

I feel that there is only one path for Australia to follow in order to achieve its full potential as a nation; that is to create a truly free enterprise economy in an independent republic.

While some improvements are slowly taking hold in Australia I would suggest the following issues must be addressed if Australia is to develop a more progressive society, a need that far outweighs any other national objectives of the late twentieth century.

Australia needs to:

#1   Secure its own national identity by declaring an Australian Republic, complete with a fully overhauled constitution based on the highest values of the freedom and rights of the individual, as embodied in the U.S. constitution and its amendments. Inseparable from the creation of a new constitution, the courts, the government, and the administration must be clearly separated and identified, with each contributing to the balance of power inside Australia.

#2   Change the voting systems at all levels of government to reflect more democratic principles (first–past–the–post with run–offs), and allow full disclosure of party allegiances on all ballot materials.

#3   Completely overhaul the infrastructure of city, state and federal bureaucracies, including a significant reduction in the membership of federal parliament and the state legislative bodies to a more manageable level.   Australia must reduce its governmental departments to an efficient and reasonable size.

#4   Remove all direct government involvement with industrial relations and wage fixing/indexation, and establish watchdog boards for the government to monitor free enterprise industrial relations. Inseparable in this process would be the transformation of the Union/Employer/Government war in industrial relations to a full collective bargaining contract based system regulated by the independent courts.   Reduce the number of public holidays, rationalize working hours and penalty rates, reduce annual leave and long–service leave allowances to levels where people have to 'earn' them.   Drastically change the approach to sick pay entitlements and introduce retirement programs that are available to the average worker.

#5   Turn all federal and state government owned and operated businesses, with the probable exception of the post office, into public companies whose stock can be purchased on the stock exchange by Australian investors before options are opened to foreign purchasers.

#6   Drastically reduce the taxation burden on all individuals from all sources including PAYE, sales and import taxes, to encourage people to work more because they will be able to keep more of what they earn.

#7 Eliminate or greatly reduce corporate taxes in order to encourage the establishment of new industries and business opportunities for all Australians.

#8 Allow the establishment of foreign banks and financial institutions, including venture capital, that can compete freely within the Australian economy.

#9 Establish an open–door, non–assisted immigration policy to which the entire world can respond. Do not offer supports and subsidies for immigrants, so only the most resourceful and capable people are attracted.

#10 Make four year college and university students pay for their education through sophisticated low–interest guaranteed loan programs and encourage the building of private colleges and universities.

It is clear that Government, Taxes, Industrial Relations, Business, Investment, Immigration and Education are the key areas of Australia's future. If only one area is left unaddressed, then Australia will not mature fully in this increasingly complex world.

I hope 'The Lucky Country' will be just that one day in the not too distant future. In the mean time, take a trip to Australia and enjoy a land and people that are both different and familiar enough to make you feel like you're a million miles from the U.S. and at the same time be treated like you are an old friend.

ANOTHER BOOK BY THE SAME AUTHOR

PLANNING YOUR FIRST VACATION TO AUSTRALIA
A Primer For The First-Time Visitor

PLANNING YOUR FIRST VACATION TO AUSTRALIA is a new, quick reference guide to help you decide on Australia as your next vacation destination.

"PLANNING..." lays out facts! The information you need BEFORE talking to your travel agent.

PLANNING YOUR FIRST VACATION TO AUSTRALIA answers these questions: So You Want To Vacation In Australia? Is It Worth My Trouble To Vacation In Australia? When Should I Travel? How Much Time Will I Need? How Much Will It Cost? Will I Be Able To Understand The Language? Where Will I Land? Is It Difficult To Travel In Australia? and many other important questions.

PLANNING YOUR FIRST VACATION TO AUSTRALIA gives brief useful facts on all states and capital cities, tells you where to get more detailed information, and finishes with 15 essential facts no visitor should be without.

The 50+ page paperback edition is $2.95 postage paid anywhere. Available from your book store or directly from A/A Publishing, P.O.Box 1772, Carmichael, Ca. 95609. See convenient order form next page.

A/A PUBLISHING ORDER FORM
POST OFFICE BOX 1772
CARMICHAEL, CA. 95609

Please send me the following books by Brian Lewis:

_____ copies of PLANNING YOUR FIRST VACATION TO AUSTRALIA @$2.95 postpaid.

_____ copies of THE NAKED AUSTRALIAN (Paperback) @$13.95 postpaid.

_____ copies of THE NAKED AUSTRALIAN (Hardcover) @$19.95 postpaid.

Please complete by printing clearly.

Name:_____

St. Address:_____

City:_____ Zip:_____

Californian residents please add the following sales tax:
PLANNING YOUR FIRST VACATION TO AUSTRALIA $0.18/copy.
THE NAKED AUSTRALIAN (paperback) $0.84/copy.
THE NAKED AUSTRALIAN (hardcover) $1.19/copy.
MAIL IMMEDIATELY WITH CHECK OR MONEY ORDER. TOTAL ENCLOSED:_____
ALLOW 4–6 WEEKS FOR DELIVERY.

Thank you for placing an order with A/A Publishing.